Praise

"David gets it. Tennis is first about fun and for teachers, how to make it fun. Learning is also best accomplished by progression. This will be a useful tool for every tennis parent and teacher looking to develop young players seriously or just introducing them to the joys of the tennis lifestyle."

CLIFF DRYSDALE

ESPN TV Analyst, Grand Slam Champion

"David Minihan's system will help you attract new players to the sport."

DR. DAVID T. PORTER,

Chairman, USPTA Player Development Advisory Council, USPTA Master Professional

"An excellent blend of innovative tennis information and guidelines which is much needed in this highly competitive tennis world."

GARY TROST

President, USPTA-Missouri Valley, Tennis Teaching Professional

"You can customize David's Progressive Plans to match your child's unique pace of tennis skill development. I only wish this book would have been available to read years ago."

PAUL LOCKWOOD

University of Oklahoma Head Coach, Men's Tennis

"I have made a career of coaching tennis and I believe David's book will help coaches teach their children to appreciate the game and keep it fun."

MARK JOHNSON

University of Oklahoma Head Coach, Women's Tennis

"David Minihan's book is a great resource for parents and coaches. With the emphasis on fun, innovative lesson plans, drills and the new QuickStart program, his book provides the tools needed to develop young players' skills that keep them on the court."

ANNE SMITH
Ph.D, Winner of 10 Grand Slam Titles

"As a former top junior and playing professional, I really like the ideas on developing a junior presented in this new book by David Minihan. This book will give a head start to all parents and coaches and be a very useful tool as it provides valuable information and insights into the world of junior tennis."

KEN FLACH
Winner of 6 Grand Slam Doubles Titles, Olympic Gold Medalist, Hall of Famer - USTA/Missouri Valley

"One of the best tennis books on the market today and every coach should read it."

JOHN NEWMAN
Former Playing Professional and Legendary coach

"Making tennis fun is the key when introducing young players to the game. David Minihan has shown us some great ways to do that in his awesome book, Coaching Your Tennis Champion."

BOB MCKINLEY
Member of 4 Tennis Halls of Fame

"Coaching Your Tennis Champion offers many games and ideas for the parents and coaches of tennis children. This resource will be great for the younger kids just picking up the racquet as it incorporates the QuickStart program geared towards younger players as well as ideas to keep tennis fun."

ANDA PERIANU
WTA Touring Professional

An Important Message to Our Readers

COACHING YOUR TENNIS CHAMPION

The Progressive Plan for Success

By David Minihan

Includes the all-new
QuickStart Tennis Format
for teaching kids tennis

*Plus! Tons of exciting new
games and coaching drills*

Mansion Grove House

Coaching Your Tennis Champion
The Progressive Plan for Success

By David Minihan
Published by Mansion Grove House
ISBN-13: 978-1-932421-15-6
ISBN-10: 1-932421-15-7

Mansion Grove House. PO Box 201734, Austin, TX 78720 USA.
Website: mansiongrovehouse.com
For information on bulk purchases, custom editions, and serial rights:
E-mail sales@mansiongrovehouse.com or write us, Attention: Special Sales.
For permission license including reprints, excerpts, and quotes:
E-mail permissions@mansiongrovehouse.com or write us, Attention: Permissions.

Printed in the United States of America

Library of Congress Cataloging-in-Publication Data
Minihan, David.
    Coaching your tennis champion : the progressive plan for success / by
David Minihan.
       p. cm.
    Includes the all-new QuickStart Tennis Format for teaching kids
    tennis. Plus! Tons of exciting new games and coaching drills.
    Includes bibliographical references and index.
    ISBN 978-1-932421-15-6 (pbk.)
    1. Tennis--Coaching. 2. Tennis for children--Coaching. I. Title.
GV1002.9.C63M56 2007
796.342--dc22
                                                              2007041992

Acquisition, Permissions, & Reviews: Kimberly Scott
Copy Editor: Jeanne Payne
Cover Design: Bill Carson
Cover Photo: Getty Images
Content Design: Eileen Llorente
Interior Photos and Diagrams: David Minihan
Marketing Development: Kelly Handel

Credits: See Appendix "Credits"

About David

David Minihan is best known for his work with "grass roots" tennis. His coaching talents and programs have been recognized by many awards from the US Tennis Association: Excellence in Tennis Programming, Outstanding Contributor to USA Team Tennis, and the USPTA Oklahoma Professional of the Year. David is the Director of Tennis at the Westwood Tennis Center, in Norman, Oklahoma— a 2007 USTA Outstanding Facility of the Year. David shares his strategies for teaching tennis and managing programs in tennis magazines and at tennis workshops. David is married to Lisa and has two daughters, Aspen and Chloe.

Contents

To my beautiful wife,
whom I love and admire,
who gave her time reviewing this book.

To my two daughters,
who inspired me to write this book.

To my mother and father
who supported all my dreams.

To my students,
whom I thank for letting me be a part
of their tennis journey.

Introduction

One day in the driveway, Adam introduced tennis to his son Sam. He knew right away that his son had the potential of being a pretty good player. Adam continued to toss balls to Sam until he got good enough to "advance" to the street and then on to the tennis court. While Adam gave him some pointers here-and-there, he believed that he needed to enroll him in some private and group lessons at our facility to further his tennis development. Adam, an accomplished player in his own right, decided not to serve as his son's coach but would still hit with him and serve as a practice partner working on what Sam learned in our progressive clinics. "Tennis has strengthened my relationship with my father because we get to spend time together and talk about life whether it is tennis related or other issues in my life. I believe I'm at the level of which I am today because of my tennis relationship with my dad and David's progressive lesson plan." Sam is one of David's most accomplished players who appears on the USTA national standings list.

There is a strong demand for a structured lesson plan geared toward the 5-10 age group among tennis professionals, junior high and high school coaches, physical education teachers and parents. There are a number of books with tennis drills available, but finding a book with progressive lesson plans is nearly impossible. The lesson plans will give you a fifteen-day progressive format which is divided up into time allotments totaling 60 minute days. The lesson plans will teach the children ground strokes, volleys, overheads and serves. In addition to drills and mechanics, the lesson plans included in this book are full of innovative and exciting games that will engage the children and produce smiles and laughter. Instructors and parents at any level will be able to implement these lesson plans, drills and games in their current program, or utilize them in starting new creative programs for their students or child.

Teaching children between ages five and ten has always been a major focus of tennis instructors throughout the world. These children are the future of tennis whether it is social or competitive play during their junior and adult years. It is our responsibility as instructors and parents to insure this age group is directed on the proper path. Is the proper path making sure they develop the correct mechanics? Proper mechanics are essential. However, it is more important to make sure they are having a blast while learning! It is essential for these children, the future of tennis, to leave each day of instruction with smiles and laughter rather than frowns and boredom.

Children between ages five and ten are more interested in having a good time and playing games than worrying about how to hold the racket and the specific techniques of hitting different strokes. Children desire to be in an atmosphere that is exciting and energetic. Mechanics are important part of training. However, we can also make it fun for the children while teaching them how to correctly hit a ball. Making this sport fun and exciting for this age group will keep them engaged and encourage them to make tennis a sport of a lifetime!

The Easy as 1-2-3 method will be introduced in this book. The Easy as 1-2-3 method simplifies the mechanics for children and allows them to experience success sooner. Too many of us focus on the players hitting the ball properly or learning modern tennis techniques too soon. While teaching proper mechanics is important, we want to make sure the emphasis is on the children having fun and enjoying the sport of tennis. Simplifying the mechanics will allow the children to enjoy the game and experience early success rather than being bored with specifics of technical issues involving mechanics. The Easy as 1-2-3 method will do just that!

The lesson plans in this book are divided up into two age divisions: Ages 5-7 and Ages 8-10. The plans are designed to progress players from the beginning of gripping a racket through the first experience of point play using the a short court format. There is a fifteen day progression with each day including one hour of games and drills. Each day the students will be working on their motor skills and developing their hand-eye coordination. Different types of equipment which aid in players' development, such as the popular fishing pole and the pee wee trainer, are utilized in these lesson plans. Most importantly, fun will be emphasized and instructors will be encouraged to make the children laugh by doing such things as wearing a funny hat with a clown nose. After all, it is all about having fun!

This book will also give parents guidance on the best practices in coaching your child as well as choosing a coach. It will be a tool in understanding the role as a parent and as a coach and help you answer the question, *"Can I be my child's coach?"*

The book also includes a chapter which contains all drills and games that appear in the lesson plans for easy reference. In addition, there are thirty additional drills and games for this age group included. All of these drills and games are designed to be fun and exciting for the players while at the same time developing their motor and tennis skills. Instructors can use these drills and games to supplement the lesson plans as they feel work well for their students.

Additional program ideas such as USTA Team Tennis Ralleyball, Olympic Tennis and Serve One Up For the Kids are also included. Adding these new programs in conjunction to the lesson plans will show the public that you have a variety of active and exiting programs to offer.

This book was not written with the intention of replacing your current programs but rather enhancing your existing programs in the hope of creating more spice and excitement for your juniors in this age group. Having a structured lesson plan full of fun games and drills is the reason we have been recognized by our USTA district and section for what we do with children ages five to ten. And now being a father of two, I know the importance of making sure my junior clinics are structured with a sound lesson plan to make sure I give them the best environment necessary in hopes they will choose tennis a sport of a lifetime.

David Minihan
E-mail: David@westwoodtennis.com

1
Keeping Kids On the Court, And Coming Back

Have you noticed how everyone is hitting the ball so hard these days? Players have this huge loop forehand, and then they close their eyes and knock the fuzz off the ball. What about on the volleys? Can you believe players today are swinging at their volleys? What happened to the simple step-and-punch volley? And what about the serve? Players now are jumping out of their shoes to hit a 110 mph serve. Crazy! My, oh my, how the game has changed! Tennis has simply turned into a power game. This change is due to racket technology and stronger, more athletic players. However, even with the game changing, we do not need to start beginner players out like the pros with mechanics such as a huge loop forehand or a swinging volley.

The goal while teaching beginners should be to make sure the players are having fun and experiencing early success. However, which mechanics to teach beginner players is often controversial. The debate often begins with groundstrokes, especially on the forehand side. Too many times players have been introduced to a huge loop forehand too early. Instructors and parents should shorten the strokes and make it easier for the player. The huge loop forehand obviously requires more motion with the arm, as a result making the timing of contact more difficult. Making it easier to learn mechanics will allow the player to experience early success.

Grip

There are five main grips in tennis: continental, eastern, hybrid, semi-western, and western. The eastern grip is the most popular grip for beginners and is most often used with forehand groundstrokes. This grip can also be used to hit backhand groundstrokes. However, I believe it is fine to begin the player using the eastern-eastern grip on the backhand, but you need to transition into the left hand as an eastern and the right hand to a continental for a right handed player. The eastern grip can also be used for volleys and serves when introducing tennis to children. However, the player will need to gradually change to a continental on the volley and serve as he develops. The eastern grip is a great grip for beginning students because it is so versatile for different strokes. There are two ways you can teach the eastern grip:

A. **Belly Button Grip** – Have the player simply put the butt of the grip to his belly button with the racket head straight up and down where he cannot see the strings. The player puts his hand flat on the strings and slides the hand down to the grip.

B. **Shake Hands Grip** – Simply shake hands with the player. Then with the butt of the racket facing the player and the head at the angle where you cannot see the strings, have him shake hands with the racket.

Along with the eastern grip, the hybrid grip is the second grip that will be used in this book. The hybrid grip is between the eastern and the semi-western grip. Lindsay Davenport uses this grip. With the hybrid grip, a player can generate greater topspin than with the eastern grip, and generate pace.

Eastern Grip

Easy as 1-2-3 Groundstrokes

Forehand

Despite the age of the beginner, introduce groundstrokes with the idea of making it as easy as 1-2-3. The stroke is simple and short and will enable players to make contact easier and faster. The following are the methods for a right-handed forehand:

Short and Sweet

1. Player begins in the traditional closed stance with his left foot in front of the right foot.

2. Easy as 1-2-3. In Position 1, the player turns his side before the ball has been fed. The racket head back points towards the fence and below his waistline. The racket head should slightly be closed while using the Eastern grip. The left hand should be out in front pointing at the ball to help with balance. The player should have a bit of flex in his knees with weight favoring the left side.

3. Easy as 1-2-3. Position 2 is the player making contact with the ball. Contact should be just in front of the left foot. Emphasize to the player to sweep up on the ball creating topspin.

4. Easy as 1-2-3. The follow through is Position 3. Have the player finish around to the left shoulder with the butt of the racket toward the other side of the court.

5. As the player progresses, add the Ready Position. Have him set up with his shoulders square to the net. Have him pivot on his right foot while at the same time moving the racket back to position 1, and stepping towards the net with his left foot. Player then goes through Positions 2 and 3.

Loopy Loop

Another way to hit the forehand is with a loop forehand. This type of forehand requires a bit more hand-eye coordination. It is important to understand, there are many factors that play in to a loop forehand such as grip, follow through, and positioning. Here are guidelines to a basic loop forehand with the hybrid grip. If you decide to teach a loop forehand to a child, make sure he doesn't use a huge loop, but one that is short and more controlled. Teaching the loop to a right-handed player:

Open Stance Forehand

1. You can begin the player with a closed stance, but I prefer to teach the player the open stance. Open up the player's stance where the left foot is not stepping towards the sideline but where the right foot is closer to the sideline.

2. The player then turns his upper body with the racket path going up and out towards the back fence down below the ball creating a loop.

3. After contact is made, the racket head should accelerate to the other side of the body on the opposite shoulder with a smooth follow through. The player should pronate their arm as the racket is coming through to the left shoulder.

Two Handed Forehand

More and more teaching professionals are beginning children with a two-handed forehand. A good friend of mine, who is a teaching professional, swears this is the best and only way we should introduce the forehand to this age group. There are two advantages to the two-handed forehand: more racket control as a result of using two hands and upper body rotation. Beginner players tend to have a "dead arm" with their off arm when hitting a regular one-handed forehand. The arm just hangs to the side as the right arm swings through the ball. The two-handed forehand will help solve that once the player progresses and releases the left arm from the racket resulting in a nice upper body rotation. When teaching the two-handed forehand to a right handed player, make sure the left hand is on top and the right hand is on bottom. This way it will be an easy transition when the player progresses and releases the left hand. The player can use either an eastern or hybrid grip with the right hand. The left hand will use an eastern grip. I would suggest you have the player bring the racket back with a small loop, but bringing the racket straight back is also fine.

Backhand

Like the forehand groundstroke, we want to make the backhand as simple as possible. There are two ways to accomplish this. The first way is to have the players use a straight-back swing with no loop, similar to Venus Williams's swing. The second way is to use a small looped swing. It aids in racket head momentum and gets the racket head below the ball, creating topspin. To begin, I would suggest you use the eastern-eastern grip to hit the two-handed backhand. Too much grip change will confuse and eventually frustrate the player. As the player develops, you will know when it is time to challenge him by rotating the grip. You will also find most players gradually change their bottom hand naturally to the continental grip. Hitting the backhand for a right-handed player:

Simple and Sweet

1. Have the player turn his side in a closed stance where his right foot is slightly closer to the sideline.
2. On the back swing Position 1, the racket goes straight back below the waistline insuring the racket head is below the ball when moving to Position 2 (hitting zone) and on to Position 3, the follow through.
3. As the racket is moving to Position 3, make sure the racket moves through smoothly to the opposite shoulder.

The professionals on television have taught us that hitting in an open stance on the backhand side is the new way to strike a backhand. I completely agree. This is a must in a player's development. However, I believe an open stance backhand is a difficult stroke for a 5-10-year-old beginner. I recommend that you begin the player with a closed stance.

You can also teach the player the loop backhand. As I suggested on the loop forehand, keep the loop small and not have the child hit a huge looping backhand.

Loopy Loop

1. Begin the player with a closed stance where the right foot is closer to the sideline.
2. The player then turns his upper body with the racket path going up and out towards the back fence and down below the ball creating a loop.
3. After contact is made, the racket head should accelerate to the other side of the body on the opposite shoulder with a smooth follow through.

Two-handed vs. one-handed: Obviously both are correct and can be taught to all levels of players. However, most beginner players are more comfortable with a two-handed backhand. The use of two hands gives them more support and allows them to feel as though they have more control. Also, 5-10-year-old players are still developing physically and lack the strength to hit a one-handed backhand correctly.

Knowing When to Change Players to Modern Mechanics

There is not a an exact point when a player should begin or transition into a loop forehand, open stance, grip change (such as semi-western grip), swinging volley or any other modern mechanic. However, changing a player to modern mechanics should come at a time when the professional feels the player is athletically and mentally ready. Changing a player's mechanics should probably come during private lessons. When you are working with groups or clinics, not everyone in that group might be ready for a particular development at the same time. Coaches should look for the following when determining to transition a child into the modern game:

1. **Hand-eye coordination:** Is the player able to see the ball bounce off the ground and make solid contact with the racket? A simple drill is tossing the ball to the player. The player can be at the service line hitting the ball. He doesn't have to be able to hit groundstrokes from the baseline to advance to the modern groundstroke.
2. **Footwork:** Is the player able to move to the ball, set his feet and make solid contact? We don't want to challenge the player with a modern groundstroke when he is hitting groundstrokes off balance and is unable to set his feet. At this point, keep the game as simple as possible. A good test drill is Hit-Recover. Feed the ball away from the player

forcing the player to move, set his feet and make contact with the ball. The player then recovers back to the center, waiting for the next ball.

3. **Mental Challenge:** Is the player ready mentally to take on challenges of the modern groundstroke? In my experience, you will find that some students might be ready physically, but not mentally. For example, I had a 10-year-old student who was a gifted athlete, whom any instructor would be excited to teach. However, the child was an extremely immature, hot-headed know-it-all. While trying to teach him the loop forehand and open stance he became frustrated. He absolutely hated it, and his temper worsened. So instead of pushing it on him, I let him stay with the straight back forehand. After showing him how my top players and professionals on tour hit their modern forehands, he wanted to change. So, instead of pushing the change on him, I let him transition into it at his own pace. By doing this and showing examples of other players, he desired the change and welcomed the challenge.

Volleys

The easiest shot in tennis for beginner players is the volley. When teaching beginners, you do not want them to have to worry about changing grips from one shot to the next. Have them use the eastern grip. As they develop, you will know when to challenge them with a grip change. Begin with the player having his side turned before the ball is fed. The use of teach feet, a rubber throw-down foot, is a great tool in aiding where the player should stand. Have the player then simply stick his racket in front of his body and punch. Do not let him swing! As he progresses, add the ready position. Have him turn by pivoting on the right foot (for a right handed player), step with the left foot, and then punch. On the backhand side, player will pivot on his left foot and step with the right foot. Have the player use two hands for stability. Have him pretend there is a brick wall behind him. Then he cannot bring the racket behind him without hitting the brick wall. A good drill is having your class line up against the fence when learning the mechanics of the volley. The fence will inhibit their backswings.

The volley is a great way to build confidence in a player. All professionals come across players who struggle with their motor skills. As a result, some players can get frustrated and even quit the sport. If you have a player who is struggling with his groundstrokes or serves, bring him up to the net and have him hit a few volleys. Have the player simply stick his racket up. Tell him not to swing. Then toss some balls at his racket. Toss them such a way that the player will not miss. Recognize that player in front of the group with a prize for being the "Best Volleyer of the Day.""

Serves

Have the player begin at the service line with his racket back on his shoulder in the "scratch back" position. We want the players to have early success and starting with the racket on his shoulder will speed up this success. The player should stand at a 45-degree angle to the net with the racket back on his shoulder as if he was going to throw a baseball. The player then throws the ball up with his non-dominate hand at one o'clock position. He then reaches up into full extension, making contact with the ball and finishes with his racket head on the opposite side of his body. A player may pull the ball down into the net or struggle to make contact with the ball. A great remedy drill is to have the player simply stop at contact and "bump" the ball over the net. Don't worry about the players having "perfect" mechanics. Have them work on making solid contact and developing their motor skills.

Diagram of one o'clock

The full motion serve should not be rushed in the development of a child's game. If any players are struggling with timing, they need to continue with their rackets on their shoulders.

When a player is ready to learn the full motion serve:

1. Player stands at a 45-degree angle to the net. (Use teach feet to help their positioning.)

2. With his racket tip pointing to the target box, the player moves the racket down to his right side (right handed player). At the same time, the non-dominant hand comes down towards their left thigh.

3. The racket now starts its way up along the right side bringing the racket head above the right shoulder. As the racket goes up, the non-dominant hand begins upward to toss the ball up. The right and left hand should be going up at the same time.

4. The right arm now needs to be in a position similar to a quarterback throwing a football. The left arm is stretched as if trying to touch the sky.

5. The player now needs to reach up to full extension to make contact.

6. After contact, the racket falls to the left side of the body.

One major mistake we can make is dwelling too much on the mechanics. Beginner players, especially ages 5-10, will get bored if they are simply standing in line working on mechanics. Juniors' attention spans are not very long. This is why it is important to change drills and games often. Don't spend a lot of time on dissecting mechanics on one particular drill. It will be noticeable in these lesson plans that the drills and games change often. Remember to make it fun for the players so they will come back and continue their development.

2
Thrilling New Ways to Make Learning Tennis Fun

Making it FUN!

A program is only as fun as you make it. Junior players in the 5–10-age range do not enjoy standing in line longer than three minutes waiting to hit two balls and then go to the end of the line. Players can learn mechanics and work on their motor skills by playing fun games and using teaching aids such as foam balls, fishing poles, and field goals. Instructors also play a huge part in making it fun for players. Instructors need to be full of energy when teaching this age group. We are ultimately the ones who are responsible for the players deciding whether they like tennis or not.

Equipment

There is a wide variety of tennis equipment on the market today to assist in making tennis fun for the younger students. The following list includes what you will need for the Easy as 1-2-3 Lesson Plan:

- **Rackets** – Every player needs a racket. Having rackets to loan players is always a good idea for those who might not have the financial means to purchase one.

- **Pee Wee "T" trainer** – This product is made out of PVC tubing that resembles a gigantic "T." It has one dangling ball on each side of the "T."

- **Cones** – Colorful cones make it more visually stimulating for the players.

- **Foam balls** – Great for developing motor skills as this oversized ball is lightweight foam for high bounce and is easy to track.

Pee Wee 'T' trainer

- **Low compression balls** – This type of ball reduces the bounce, thus giving children better control, but maintains the liveliness of the ball. These balls usually come in a two-tone color.

- **Funny hat** – A funny hat entertains the players, and they can use it for target practice as well.

- **Field goal** – This product is also made out of PVC tubing. Players will enjoy having a huge target to hit through as the pro yells, "Field goal!"

- **Bean bags**

- **Clown nose**

- **Hula hoop**

- **Flat targets** or "spots"

- **Lines** separating the lines using roll-down lines or tape for 36' or 60' courts.

The Fishing Pole

- **Fishing pole** – This is a fantastic aid for teaching the serve and overhead. This device is a 5' pole with a ball at the end of a dangling string attached to the pole. On some poles, the ball doesn't come off after contact. Other poles have Velcro® attached at the end of the string where you can attach a ball. After a player hits it, the ball separates from the string. Some people refer to it as the "serving doctor." You will be able to use this for groundstrokes, volleys, and serves.

- **Teach feet**

- **Rallyball score sheet**

- **Radio**

- **Racket net** - Take an old 21"- 23"- or 25" racket and cut out the strings. Get a basketball net and attach the net to the frame of the racket as if the racket head is the rim of a basket. Tie off the bottom of the net so it will catch the ball.

- **5' Fishing Net** – You can get this at any sporting goods store. It's great for target practice.

5' Fishing Net

Other Successful Teaching Tools

- **Teaching cable** – This cord connects from one fence to another with dangling balls. It helps while working on the player's groundstrokes and volleys.
- **Balloons**
- **Beach balls**
- **Ball machine**
- **Line targets**
- **Streamer balls**
- **Mini nets**

Teaching tools keep it FUN!

You can find most of the above equipment through major tennis manufacturers. The terminology in this book may differ with some manufacturer's products. Companies often come out with teaching aids that are similar but they are labeled differently. You can also make many of the above teaching aids to save money. The pee wee trainer, fishing pole, and field goal can all be made out of PVC tubing. It's very inexpensive and can be found at your local hardware store.

Using teaching aids to help teach your students is important for the success of your program. Kids will enjoy using aids such as the field goal and fishing pole. They'll get a kick out of seeing you in a funny hat. The equipment is a vital part of the kids having fun and laughing. They also visually stimulate the kids interest and they will ask themselves, "I wonder what that is for?" We have had many parents ask where they can buy low-compression balls, fishing poles or other teaching devices. As a result, we began to special order teaching aids for parents. These parents used these aids when helping their child practice what they learned in their past lesson.

Ensuring your students have the proper racket in their hand is extremely important for their success on the court. Children can become frustrated if they are having a hard time making contact with the ball because the racket is either too heavy or too long. It is common to have a player come to your program with a wooden racket. If a player shows up with a wooden racket, loan her a racket that fits. Usually after one day of practice, the parents will purchase a new racket for their child. The parents will appreciate you caring about their child enough to have the correct racket in her hand. The advance of technology available helps young children achieve success earlier when utilized. The following is a good guideline on how to fit your student with a racket according to height and age:

Racket Length	Student Height	Age
21″	height 40-44″	or age 4+
23″	height 45-49″	or age 6+
25″	height 50-55″	or age 8+
26″	height 60″	or age 12+

From Head® Racquets

Recognition with Prizes

Kids love to receive praise from the coach, whether it is a "high five" or a prize. Positive reinforcement is the key to instructing children, and prizes are a great way to accomplish this. Prizes add spice to the program and keep the children interested and motivated. Recognition really is essential in making your program a success. There is nothing more rewarding than seeing the look on a player's face when receiving a prize for her achievement. She will be excited to tell her parents that she earned a prize! Even after a lesson with my daughter, she can't wait to get off the court and collect her hard-earned taffy candy. The following are some ideas for prizes:

- Candy (no gum!)
- Colorful pencils
- T-shirts
- Stickers
- Coloring books for the younger children
- Trophies
- Certificates
- Tennis bag
- New tennis racket

At the end of each session, prizes should be given to everyone. Children can have a great time during the day or even throughout the session, but if their friends get prizes and they do not, it can spoil the entire program for them. Make sure everyone leaves your tennis facility with a prize! It's a good idea to have a party at the end of the session. You can make it a pizza, ice cream, snow cone, cake, or simply a soda party.

Recognizing players with prizes, "high-fives," and verbal praise should be used in your programs to make everyone feel good about themselves. Without positive reinforcement, professionals are doing a disservice to their students. It is vital that you recognize all players with prizes.

Some ideas for recognizing your child on the tennis court:

- Good contact with the ball. The ball does not even need to make it into the court or into a specific target area. Simply recognizing the player for good contact gets a child excited.
- Good follow through
- Nice hustle to the ball
- Brushing up on the ball creating topspin
- Good extension on the serve
- Great attitude in today's practice
- Winning a game or drill
- Fantastic footwork
- Great work ethic
- Skills chart winner

Instructors and Parent-Coaches

This is where the fun begins. A lot of drills and games are only as fun as the instructor and parent make them. For five-to-ten year olds, the instructors and parents need to be energetic, vocal, and patient. Instructors need to have a passion for teaching junior tennis. Children respond well with instructors and parents who can make them smile, laugh, and have a great time.

Instructors will make a huge impression on children. We all remember certain schoolteachers that stood out from the rest whether they were good or bad. I will always remember my personal coach growing up. He was always encouraging whether I was in a slump or winning matches. He is the reason that I am a teaching professional today. We do not want the students to remember the sport of tennis as being a bad experience because their instructor or parent had a poor attitude. If an instructor's attitude is negative, it may have a long-term affect on the players' participation in tennis. Make sure all instructors are energetic, look players in the eye, smile, laugh, and offer plenty of positive reinforcement!

Equipment, recognizing players' achievements, and quality instructors are all extremely important for the success of your program. Say good-bye to the days of players standing in line, hitting four balls, and having the instructor say nothing or something in a boring tone. Using fun equipment, giving out tons of prizes, and having an energetic instructor will be beneficial to your program and will hopefully inspire players to make tennis the sport of a lifetime!

3
Have You Tried QuickStart Tennis? Plus, More Smashing Programs!

The Easy as 1-2-3 lesson plans serve as the groundwork for a professional's junior programs or coaching your child. You can expand these programs with other activities that will keep the excitement fresh for your students. As fun as you make your tennis clinics or experience with your child, it can get boring for the players who repeat these programs over and over. Adding different and creative programs for this age group will help to keep their interest in tennis and keep them coming back to the court. Such programs can include USTA Jr. Team Tennis, with QuickStart Tennis, Olympic Tennis and Serve One Up For the Kids.

QuickStart Tennis

According to a 6-year-old junior player in an *Austin American-Statesman*, article, "Some bigger courts are hard to hit good shots. The small courts help me play with my friends."

QuickStart Tennis is focused on the age group 10 and under. Because this age group's stride length and arm span is not as long as an adult's, this format focuses on shortening the tennis court. It shortens the court size for ages 8 and under to 36' x 18' and for ages 10 and under to 60' x 21' for singles play and to 60' x 27' for doubles play. Expecting children ages 10 and under to cover a full size court is nearly impossible. The shortened court is more proportional to their body size. Other QuickStart modifications include a lower net, low-compression and foam balls, and proper racket size. This type of format has been long overdue and I applaud USTA for launching this great concept. QuickStart Tennis is based on six key elements:

1. Court size
2. Net height
3. Age
4. Ball speed and weight
5. Racket size
6. Scoring

"Hopefully courts this size will help kids gravitate toward tennis at an earlier age. It will make it a little bit easier to use the skills that are needed to play tennis without battling the size issues."

Andy Roddick, 2003 US Open Champion,
Quoted in Austin American-Statesman, July 20. 2007

In other sports aimed at the younger players, we see basketball with a shorter goal, baseball with T-ball, and soccer and football with shorter fields. All of these modifications make the game simpler for the children. It's the same with QuickStart Tennis. Below is breakdown of the QuickStart format:

Age	Court Size	Racket	Ball	Net Height	Scoring
8 years and under	36' x 18'	Up to 23"	Foam ball	2'9"	Best of three games 1st to 7 point games
10 years and under	60' x 21' singles 60' x 27' doubles	Up to 25"	Orange low compression balls	3'	Best of 3 sets of 1st to 4 games, with 3rd set 1st to 7 points

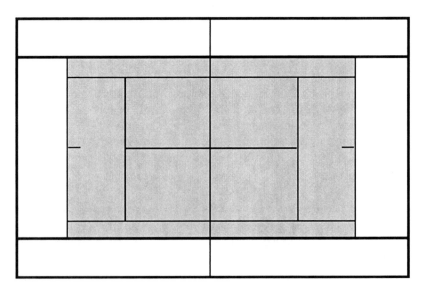

60' Court Layout

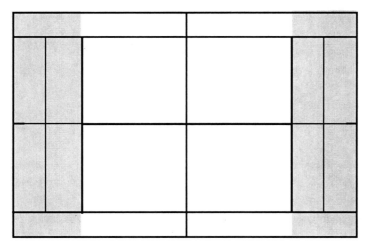

36' Court Layout

OR

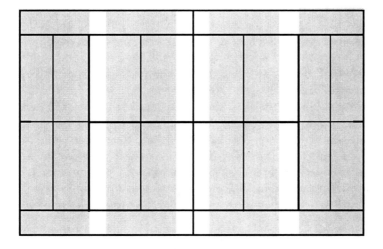

36' Court Layout

The QuickStart 36' court is great for instructors when teaching large groups with limited court availability. One regulation court can serve up to four 36-foot courts.

According to the USTA, the key goals of QuickStart Tennis are to:

- Increase the number of beginning players ages 5 to 10
- Increase the retention of players ages 5 to 10 and beyond
- Improve the technical, tactical and physical development of players ages 5 to 10
- Develop future champions
- Improve the wellness of youth playing tennis

"The USTA is proud to have assisted with the design and construction of the first permanent 60-foot courts in the country. It is with great pleasure they are here at the exquisite Horseshoe Bay Resort."

Virgil H. Christian, USTA Director of Community Development
Quoted in Austin American-Statesman, July 20. 2007

Horseshoe Bay Resort in Horseshoe Bay, Texas is home to the Andy Roddick USTA Kids' Courts, the first specifically designed 10 and under tennis courts. Juniors ages 10 and under can now play on 60-foot courts.

I highly recommend this format for all teaching professionals and parents. This format will be implemented in USTA tournaments and USTA Jr. Team Tennis. You will find in the progression lesson plans that all instructional drills and games are short courts whether the player is instructed on the service line or a few feet back. The plans never expand the 78' feet from baseline to baseline. Using shortened courts, the correct balls, and the proper-sized rackets are vital for the early success for the 10-and-under age group! For more on this program, visit www.partners.quickstarttennis.com. Visit your local tennis pro shop for information on purchasing the proper equipment for this program. All major manufacturers will be carrying the short court equipment.

"Project 36/60 (QuickStart Tennis) will serve to introduce, educate and encourage children of our members and guests to play the great game of tennis."

Michael Thomas, Horseshoe Bay Resort President and COO,
Quoted in Austin American-Statesman, July 20. 2007

USTA Team Tennis Ralleyball

Ralleyball is a fantastic program that you can easily branch off from the Easy as 1-2-3 progressive lesson plans. Children enjoy playing team organized sports such as little league baseball, soccer, or basketball. Children enjoy playing team sports because they enjoy the team atmosphere where they can be with friends and making new ones. And they enjoy taking what they have learned in practice and implementing it in a game. Ralleyball allows children to have both of these experiences.

Ralleyball was designed to reward players with one point for making a shot over the net and into the court rather than rewarding a point based on playing out a traditional point. The program operates by forming a league of three or more teams with approximately four to six players per team. Hire staff members or have parents volunteer their time to be a coach of a team. Each team has one practice per week for 45 minutes. Pick a day of the week to be match day. Just like the practice, the match will again take approximately 45 minutes. Recruit a parent to volunteer as a score-keeper on match day. The match format consists of having two players on each service line in doubles formation. Each time a player hits the ball over the net and into the court he scores one point for his team. If the other team rallies the ball back over the net and into the court, it receives one point, and so on. The coach feeds the ball to the first player. If the player misses

Kids love the team atmosphere of ralleyball

the first feed, they get a second feed. After the rally is over, the players on both teams rotate. One player moves off the court, the partner moves over a spot and the next player in line comes on the court. After each player from one team gets fed a ball, the opposing team gets the feeds. Each set is a ten-minute set. Whoever has the most points at the end of the ten minutes wins the set. Play all three sets even if one team wins the first two sets.

I directed a national pilot for this program and I have to say, that next to our progressive lesson plans, this is by far one of our most popular programs. It allows beginners to play tennis in a competitive team environment. Every season, we have many parents and children asking what other programs they can sign up for after the completion of ralleyball. It is a great way to introduce tennis and educate parents on your current and upcoming junior tennis programs. To learn more about this program, you can go to www.usta.com.

Olympic Tennis

Olympic Tennis focuses on motor skills as well as the players' mechanics in an atmosphere filled with excitement and prizes. Use with beginners, ages 5-12. You can hire a staff or ask for volunteers to monitor each "Olympic" event. Each event awards a ribbon to the gold, silver, and bronze winners. Place five to seven players in a group. Each station is timed 10-15 minutes. The specific time of each station will be up to you while you determine how many players you have. Since there are only three ribbons handed out in each event, have the instructor ask a couple of trivia questions at the end of the event for prizes. Make sure you give the players who did not win a ribbon the first chance to answer the questions. You want to make sure everyone leaves with a prize. The following are some ideas of "Olympic" events:

- **Bump up and bump down relays**–Bumping up consists of the player taking the racket with his palm up and bumping the ball up. Bumping down is when the player takes the racket with his palm down bumping the ball down. The goal is to control the ball where it isn't bouncing erratically.
- **Sandwich relays**–This is when you divide the group into teams. Each team will pair up. One player will have the ball on their racket, palm up. Their partner will sandwich the ball with their racket, palm down. They work together as a team to a target and then tag the next pair in line. First team to complete the relay wins!
- **Tennis basketball**–Set up a hula hoop and have the players hit volleys into the hula hoop. Players get a point for each ball hit into the hula hoop.
- **Field Goal!**–Players hit groundstrokes. If a player hits successfully in the field goal, he gets one point.
- **Serves**–Players serve from the QuickStart baseline and get one point for successfully hitting the ball into the proper box.

This is a great event to do for birthday parties or fundraisers. If you market Olympic Tennis well, you can raise a lot of funds with this fun event and create exciting parties. The program can last one hour or longer depending on how many players you have and how much you want to charge each player.

Serve One Up For the Kids

Serve One Up For the Kids uses stations of different events, similar to Olympic Tennis. This event is great for all juniors ages 5-18 and all abilities. The main difference is that every player wins all kinds of prizes. To make this program a success, get sponsors to aid you in supplying an unlimited amount of prizes. Each player is given a bag at the beginning of the program to collect the prizes that he wins in each station. To kick the program off, spread out prizes on one half of the court. Form two lines feeding one ball to each line by alternating feeds. When a player hits one of the prizes, he wins it! After ten to fifteen minutes, divide the players into groups and send them off to different stations. Each station is a game or some sort of competition such as tennis baseball. Hire staff or volunteers to serve as the instructors for this program. Have bags of candy at all stations to give out to the players after they complete a station. Give out an additional prize for the player who wins that station's event. Some prize ideas:

- Candy (no gum)
- Colorful pencils
- New tennis racket
- Tennis balls
- Tennis bag
- Grip tape
- Shock dampeners
- Coupons to pizza restaurants
- Coupon to the movies
- T-shirts

This program can also serve as a fundraiser with the proper preparation and sponsorships. If you use this program as a fundraiser you will need to charge the players a fee. However, Serve One Up For the Kids is also a great way to promote tennis and try to attract new kids to the sport by not charging a fee.

Wilson® Nights

Sally Schwartz, USPTA and PTR professional with Canyon Creek Club in Richardson, Texas, has developed a program that has proven successful called Wilson® Nights. This program was developed with the idea of continuing the player's match play development. While instructors encourage their players to play many tournaments to gain match-play experience, many of those players do not win a match, and therefore they are in and out in just 2-4 hours.

While playing tournaments are important and programs like Wilson® Nights are not substitutions. They are aids to help continue the mucneeded match play experience, while having fun in the process. Players participate in this program from 6:30 pm – 10:30 pm. The program is for entry-level tournament players through advanced tournament players of all ages. Players are matched together based on ability. They play one set with no ad scoring. For the next round, winners are paired together and losers of the previous match are paired together. This format continues for future rounds. Sally says her goal is that "everyone leaves where they at least win two sets." They play singles until 9:30 pm, then they are paired together and play doubles for one hour. Free t-shirts, provided by Wilson®, are given to each player, along with all-you-can-eat snacks. A prize drawing completes the program. "Players come out, have a great time, and get challenged. It is parent-friendly as the parents can go to dinner and catch a movie," Sally said.

Ralleyball Score Sheet

Match Date _____

Team Points_____Set #1

1	2	3	4	5
6	7	8	9	10
11	12	13	14	15
16	17	18	19	20
21	22	23	24	25
26	27	28	29	30

Team Points_____Set #1

1	2	3	4	5
6	7	8	9	10
11	12	13	14	15
16	17	18	19	20
21	22	23	24	25
26	27	28	29	30

Team Points_____Set #2

1	2	3	4	5
6	7	8	9	10
11	12	13	14	15
16	17	18	19	20
21	22	23	24	25
26	27	28	29	30

Team Points _____Set #2

1	2	3	4	5
6	7	8	9	10
11	12	13	14	15
16	17	18	19	20
21	22	23	24	25
26	27	28	29	30

Team Points _____Set #3

1	2	3	4	5
6	7	8	9	10
11	12	13	14	15
16	17	18	19	20
21	22	23	24	25
26	27	28	29	30

Team Points_____Set #3

1	2	3	4	5
6	7	8	9	10
11	12	13	14	15
16	17	18	19	20
21	22	23	24	25
26	27	28	29	30

4
Former Top Rank Player: Can You Be Your Child's Coach?

There is a point in your child's development when it would be a good idea to hand off your child's instruction to a teaching professional. Parents can actually hurt a player's development if they are stubborn and feel as though they can personally take her to the next level, which could be tournament play and/or collegiate tennis. In addition, as a child gets older, she has a tendency not to listen to parents and/or believe anything they say—even if the parents are right, or even qualified. Below are some guidelines that might be helpful in determining when to hand off your child to a certified teaching professional:

- **Understanding your limitation as an instructor.** What level did you play competitive tennis? If you never played tournaments, you probably will be challenged in understanding the mental aspect of the game. For example, it would be challenging to know how the player feels inside when it is 6-5 in the third set and she just doubled fault on match point. A certified professional will have the necessary experience to help a player handle issues that might arise during a match.

- **Wishing to be a parent rather than a coach.** *How was your day? Did you have fun? Would you like something to eat?* Gary Trost's mother would ask him these questions after junior tennis tournaments when he was a child. Gary is now Director of Tennis at the prestigious Oklahoma City Golf and Country Club. Instead of first asking Gary, "Did you win?" she was more concerned about how her son's day went and whether he had fun at the tennis tournament. Gary's mother was an accomplished player in her own right winning numerous Australian Junior Open titles. She did not serve as her son's coach, but rather chose to serve as solely

> *"As a junior competitive player, my mom was definitely lacking the positive parent role when it came to tennis. Her first question to me would be, "Did you win?" instead of "How was your day?" or "Did you have fun?" It was extremely stressful. It was even more stressful to know that she would have plenty more comments if I didn't win."*
> A Former Competitive Junior

a parent and to provide Gary what he needed to be successful in life. Sometimes it can be difficult and stressful enjoying your child's tennis while serving both roles. Children often need a parent's shoulder to lean on rather than the parent serving as a coach. While a parent can do both, it is a difficult task.

- **Your child is not responding to you as a coach.** If this is the case, you need to search for a teaching professional. You don't want to hurt your parent-child relationship or risk your child resenting the sport if you continue as the coach.

There are many good players that have had their parents as their coach from age five up to the college or professional level. One such example is Jimmy Connors who was coached by his mother, Gloria Connors. Jimmy Connors won eight singles grand slam tournaments, as well as reaching number one in the world for 160 consecutive weeks. However, in my experience, this type of relationship is rare and represents a very small percentage.

Consider your role to be one of introducing tennis to your child and determining if tennis is a sport she wishes to and should pursue. You play a key role in your child determining whether or not she likes tennis. Your child might not even like tennis and as hard as that might be for you to accept, it is something you must respect. The parent needs to remember that his or her goal is for tennis to be a sport that the child will want to play for a lifetime. This may mean reintroducing the sport at a later time. The child may not like it at the age of seven, but may love the game at the age of fifty. You want the child to have great memories of the lessons they had with their mom or dad. By creating great memories, you and your child will benefit from these memories for years to come. Below are some guidelines that will be helpful for parents playing a role in their child's development:

- Provide a shoulder to lean on. Let her know you are there for her when she needs you, rather than being too involved.
- Listen to your child. After a match, let your child come to you to talk about the match as she needs time to cool down. When your child expresses burn-out, do not keep pushing tennis on her but rather have her take a break.
- Present tennis to your child as an opportunity, not as an obligation. Let her choose whether she would like to pursue tennis.
- Avoid the "We's." For example: "We didn't have a good tournament," or "We didn't make enough first serves." Your role should be one of support. You are not the one hitting the balls and playing the matches.
- Give your child options other than tennis. Children need to experience other activities to aid in their development as a child.
- When choosing a coach for your child, choose one that you feel can develop your child's tennis, and will serve as a great role model. Also, look for professionals who are certified through the USPTA or PTR.

- Be a role model for your child. Avoid verbally attacking other parents, referees or tournament directors. Do not approach your child's opponent unless you are telling them they played a great match.
- Provide financial means and transportation for your child's tennis.
- The only expectation you should have for your child is that she is enjoying tennis and is exhibiting exceptional sportsmanship.
- Many tennis players look over to their mom and dad during tournament matches. Make sure after your child loses a point, you do not exhibit negative emotions whether it is by facial expressions, getting up and walking away, or by verbalizing something negative.
- If you hired a coach, do not stand over the coach as she is working with your child. Let the coach do her job and coach.

Choosing the Right Coach

Look for a professional who gives a lot of praise, who is energetic, and who emphasizes tennis in a fun environment. Look for a professional who has the ability to teach different methods to find which one would best fit your child. For instance, there are some professionals who strictly teach a straight-back forehand. This type of forehand might not work best for your child. Teaching professionals need to be able to adjust their mechanics to fit each child.

When choosing the right coach, consider seeing if she is certified through either the USPTA or PTR. While there are great coaches who are not certified, you can be assured that an instructor who is certified has gone through the necessary steps to be a quality teaching professional. They have been trained on how to teach and handle children.

Once you have found a coach, consider watching your child's private lessons from a distance or not to watch at all. Often professionals have found parents to be a distraction to the children. Sometimes children get upset when they look over to their parents and see them have some type of negative expression after missing a shot. The coach and the child also need to create a bond where the child can open up to the

> *"The best advice I can give to a parent is to take them to the best pro they can. The kid has to be happy and with the parent there to support their child and send them to a teaching professional, this can be done."*
> Phil Dent,
> former top ATP Professional

coach and be honest about how she is feeling. For instance, a child might be willing to tell her coach she is getting burned out on tennis, whereas telling her mom or dad might upset them. In this case, the coach can inform the parents when their child needs to lay off from tennis for a predetermined amount of time. Also, by being on the court watching your child, you could make the teaching professional nervous. This could affect the way he or she teaches. As hard as it is to stay away, your child will improve faster by letting the teaching professional coach your child in a parent-free environment.

Group Lesson vs. Private Lesson

Every child is different in the way they respond to instruction. Some might prefer a group setting rather than one-on-one lessons. In group settings, there are a lot more games available that kids can enjoy. In addition, your child might enjoy the lesson better if she is with her friends. Children who watch their peers play tennis also are eager to copy them or have a desire to do better than them. I was teaching my daughter to play and had a hard time getting her to follow through. I got her in a group setting, she watched her peers and followed through like a champ. I could not believe that all it took was for her to be in a group setting to understand.

> *"I loved going to lessons with my coach when I was younger; it was one of my favorite parts of junior tennis."*
>
> A Former Competitive Junior

There are also children who do not enjoy the group setting for any number of reasons. Maybe they are shy or easily intimidated. In addition, a private setting is always nice to be able to spend personal time with your student to strengthen your relationship. However, a parent needs make sure he or she isn't being demanding on the child but rather making sure the child is having fun.

My Child is Losing Interest in Tennis

If it hasn't happened, it will. Your child will get a little burned out on tennis. The key is not letting it happen often , but only a few times. You want the child to be hungry for tennis. When she begins to lose a little interest in the sport, you need to back off, let her breathe and sign up for different activities. Taking a break from tennis would be the first step. Often a layoff can create a desire to get back on the court.

As bad as we hate to say it, tennis might not be their sport. The important thing is that you do not push the issue, but rather let them come to you asking to play. Remember, we want the kids to play tennis the rest of their lives and not hate the sport when they are adults.

Changing environments might also help. That means you might want to enroll them in a junior program at your local club or take private lessons from a certified teaching professional. Your child might also enjoy tennis more if you allow him or her to ask a friend to come with them during a lesson.

The worse thing a parent can do is force tennis or any sport on their child. You are hurting their chances of progressing as a player or even enjoying the sport. A parent's role is to give their child the opportunity to play tennis. If the child does not want to play, that is her right, so move on and hope she decides that she wants to play again in the future.

Conclusion

Parents need to create a positive and supportive environment for their child. This goes for any sport your child plays. Become a good listener. Let your child vent to you when she is frustrated by the way she is playing. Do not emphasize winning or the end result of a match. Rather be one who will give your child a hug when they lose and a high-five when they win. Show them unconditional love, win or lose.

The Ten Commandments for the Tennis Parent
How to be the best tennis parent ever!

1. **Be a positive role model for your child. Children tend to imitate their parents.** This includes not making a scene when your child is not playing well during a practice session or a private lesson with their coach. Also, during tournament play, do not get upset at your child for the way they played, especially in front of other players and parents. And finally, be kind to the tournament directors, umpires, and other parents.

2. **Provide a shoulder for your child to lean on when they are not playing well when they just lost a match.** After a match your child just lost, it is not best to approach him or her right away and offer advice. Rather let your child cool off. Wait for him or her to talk to you about the match. Rather than offer negative criticism, focus on positive feedback and encourage your child. Let your child's coach offer the majority of the advice and evaluations.

3. **Do not offer suggestions to your child's coach on how to coach. You are paying your child's coach to coach.** It is difficult for a coach to relax and develop a relationship with the child if she feels the parent is always looking over her shoulder and offering advice on how to coach the child.

4. **Do not become an overzealous parent.** A parent should not have a desire to control every single aspect of his or her child's tennis development. Do not live through your child to meet goals that you were not able to meet when you were a child.

5. **Leave the tennis teaching on the court, don't take it home.** My former assistant pro told me a story about her father teaching her. When she completed practice with her father, they would go home and she would have to write 100-500 sentences on how she would correct her mistakes like, "I will always follow through on my forehand." This is an extreme example, but parents need to leave the coaching on the court.

6. **Let your child's instructor coach in a parent-free environment.** Watch your child's lessons from a distance or don't watch at all. If you do watch your child's lesson, watch from outside the fence.

7. **Have your child thank their coach and tournament director after the lesson or tournament.** I will never forget running a National Open when a player was just eliminated from the tournament losing a close match. He came up to me with tears in his eyes thanking me for running a good event. It meant a lot to me not only getting a compliment, but how much it impressed me that a boy that just lost a tough match and was probably embarrassed because he was crying, made a point to shake my hand and thank me.

8. **Let your child participate in other sports and activities.** Do not make tennis their only activity in their life. They need other activities in their life not only to aid in physical and mental development, but also to explore other interests.

9. **Teach your child sportsmanship.** It is our responsibility as parents to insure our children exhibit good sportsmanship. Such things as making the correct calls, shaking your opponent's hand after a match, not talking "trash" to your opponent, and simply saying, "good match" after a match would be a few examples of sportsmanship.

10. **If you can't say anything positive to your child while teaching or at the end of a match, don't say anything at all.** One of my students just upset the number one seed. Coming off the court, the opponent walked over to his father with his head down and dejected. The father then began to yell at him telling him how poorly he played and how he could not believe that was the type of performance his money was paying for. I felt bad for the child as he was sobbing on the way to the car. This absolutely was not good for a child to hear from his parent, especially when the child was only ten years old. Be positive or don't say anything at all.

5
Making the Next Tennis Weekend with Your Child Unforgettable

A child learning to play tennis from his parent can be a rewarding experience for both the parent and child. The number one challenge for a parent teaching a child is the possibility the child might not respond well to there instruction. This chapter will aid in creating a positive parent-child environment and help you understand when to teach your child and when to hand your child over to a tennis professional.

A parent's number one goal in teaching a child should be to introduce tennis as a sport to enjoy for a lifetime. If the parent expects the child to become successful overnight, there will be some serious issues as to whether the child will even enjoy tennis. However, if a parent can make the game fun, the child will want to return to the court and spend more time with the parent, thus building a stronger relationship between the parent and child.

Challenges for Parents Teaching Their Child

Challenge #1:
You may discover that your child does not respond well to you teaching him tennis, no matter how much you know about the sport. I have tried to give my daughter private lessons and she does not respond well to me—and I've been in the business for years. I understand that continuing on this path could lead to her frustration and resentment for the game.

Solution:
First, focus on making sure your child is having fun. In my case, when I teach my daughter, I make sure she is having fun and focus on fun activities rather than focusing on the mechanics. I would rather delay her development as a player than have her quitting tennis because I was too stubborn. Keep your lessons short with the goal to get your child wanting more. Consider your time with him as a chance for a bonding experience which he will remember positively for years to come.

Challenge #2:
Your voice or your facial expressions show frustration when your child is not hitting properly or has performed poorly in a match.

Solution:

A child knows when he did not perform well in a match. He doesn't need to come off the court to see his parent upset or voicing displeasure in the way he played. Though I have had some students whose parents get upset, I have had more parents give their child a hug after a loss or after a poor practice performance. Your child will respond better to you as his coach when you give more hugs and less frowns.

This also goes when teaching your child. Make sure when instructing to always end on a positive note. Sometimes when teaching beginners, we have a tendency to focus on the negatives of the mechanics, rather than to focus on the positives.

Challenge #3:

My child is getting bored in our lessons.

Solution:

This often happens not only with parents teaching their child, but also with certified professionals teaching a player. You need to spice things up, whether it is introducing a new teaching aid device or wearing a funny hat. Shorten your lessons and change your lesson plans. Keep them guessing with excitement on what's next! Also, consider enrolling your child in group tennis clinics where they can play with children their own age.

Challenge #4:

I am struggling to get my child to hit the ball properly.

Solution:

Getting your child to hit groundstrokes, volleys or serves correctly can sometimes, to say the least, be a challenge. One solution is to take a break from that particular stroke for a few days—maybe even a few weeks—and give the child something else to focus on. You may also consider it the right time to enroll your child with a certified teaching professional for private lessons.

Challenge #5:

Leave your coaching on the court; do not take it home.

Solution:

This will be a challenge as you will be tempted to discuss your child's tennis at home. It is important to be a parent at home and be a coach on the court. I had a player whose parent served as her coach at a young age. She told me how her mom would constantly discuss her tennis with her at home and as a result drew her further and further from tennis. She said she enjoyed her time with her mom on the court as a coach, but missed her mom in the house as a mother.

Lesson Length

There are a couple of factors in considering how long your lesson should be with your child. First, you need to recognize when your child is getting bored. Their eyes might begin wandering. They might not be responding to you as they were in the beginning of the lesson. At this point, you need to pack it up and call it a day. If you keep grinding and forcing them to play, they will begin to dislike the sport and not want to come back.

Second, consider stopping the lesson when your child is having a great time. End the lesson on a positive note where he wants to come back for more! You want him to be hungry for tennis.

Remember, tennis is merely another form of entertainment. Tennis is in competition with other sports as well as video games, computers, cartoons, and dance. We want our kids to choose tennis as their lifetime sport. We don't want them to burn out and choose another competitor over tennis. Be smart on the length of the lesson and keep it short and fun.

Patience! Patience! Patience!

If you do not have any experience teaching tennis or another sport to young children, it can challenge your patience. Sometimes we forget as parents that children are not trying to hit the ball the wrong way. Parents can get frustrated and sometimes angry when their child is not responding well to their instruction. Take a deep breath and remember that the primary goal is to in-

> *"There were many times after a practice with my father, I would not speak to him at home because of the frustration he showed while teaching me."*
>
> A former junior competitor.

sure your child is enjoying tennis and his time with you. If you are showing your frustration and taking it out on him, you are damaging his chances of wanting to continue to play tennis, as well as the parent-child relationship. If you are having a difficult time controlling your frustration, you need to consider calling your local professional to begin giving your child lessons.

Introducing the Mechanics

When teaching your 5–10-year-old child, make sure you are stressing the *positives* of his mechanics, even if the child misses the ball completely. It is always important to end your instruction on a positive note, rather than emphasizing the negative of the stroke. For instance, your child, "Billy," hits a forehand groundstroke which results in the ball going into the bottom of the net. Instead of saying, "Billy, I have told you over and over not to hit the ball high-to-low, but rather low-to-high, listen to me!" a better response would be, "Man, what great contact! Try to get the racket a little lower so you can clear the net. Give me a high-five for making great contact!" Ending on a positive note and being energetic with that positive note will help the child want to learn and listen to your instruction.

Remember, making it easy for your child is extremely important. Instead of focusing on the specifics of his mechanics, focus more on hand eye coordination and motor skills. Play a lot of games and use a lot of teaching aids to help him understand the mechanics. By doing this and being energetic and excited when teaching, you can be sure that he is having fun.

Make it Fun!

Teaching tennis in a fun and exciting environment is extremely important in order for your child to enjoy tennis and have that desire to come back. Use innovative ways in teaching him, such as wearing a funny hat or using different teaching aid equipment. If your child is not having fun and you are having a hard time communicating in a fun way, consider enrolling your child in your local club's junior programs.

Following the lesson plans in this book and teaching aid suggestions will keep your lessons exciting and new. Simply wearing a clown's nose can add spice to the lesson. If you see that your child is getting bored in the lesson, try to introduce a new teaching aid in the next lesson. Remember, you want to experience quality time with your child and you want to insure he is having a good time.

6
Building an All-Star Team

Once you have decided to enroll your child in junior programs or take private lessons from a certified teaching professional, it is now a team effort in insuring that she is guided on the right road in her tennis development. The coach, parent, and child need to be able to communicate openly about issues concerning the child's development.

Goals and Expectations

The expectations and goals of a child might differ from those of her parent and of her coach. These need to be talked about so the team—child, coach, parent—understands and works towards the various goals. The tennis development might be one of simply playing tennis casually with friends and taking private lessons for fun, or it could be a development of playing tournament tennis.

A parent's goal for a child to play professional tennis might not be the goal of the child. The percentage of a child developing into a professional player is very small. There are many factors that must happen for a child to develop the type of game to play professionally. A coach needs to be able to help guide his students to obtain realistic goals. Parents need to accept whatever goal their child has and support her, regardless of their expectations.

Good Parents Gone Bad

There are some parents who are overzealous in regard to their child's tennis. They make all the decisions for their child and never let the child take on any responsibility for herself. This type of parent also has a tendency to tell the coach what he needs to work on with the child rather than letting the coach make those decisions for himself. There is danger that the child could show resentment for the sport and the parent.

There is also the type of parent who is physically or mentally abusive to his child. It is sad to watch a parent yell and scream at his child for not playing well in a match. At one national event in the United States, a player came off the court just winning a close match. The parent approached the child that won and began yelling at her telling her she should have won the match 6-0, 6-0. By this time, everyone around was watching her father mentally abuse the child as she was on her knees crying. The tournament officials had to call the police to control the parent. While this sounds like an extreme case, this type of behavior happens all the time.

How do we, as parents, avoid being overzealous? Recently, the USTA released the results of its study, "Understanding the Role Parents Play in Junior Tennis Success." The USTA defines early years as "the beginning phase of a child's tennis development where he or she develops a strong liking of the game. Participation is often recreational with very little systematic training." In the study, players, parents, and coaches indicated several positive parental behaviors.

Positive Parental Behaviors in the Early Years:
- Provides transportation
- Provides emotional, logistical, and financial support
- Provides the opportunity and resources
- Provides push to play, but does not pressure
- Exhibits emotional control
- Emphasizes fun
- Stresses good on-court conduct
- Helps develop child's talents by hitting with child (and sometimes coaching)

The majority of parents have good intentions in helping their child's dream come true. The best thing a parent can do after introducing tennis to their child is to hire a certified professional to take over the child's development and offer support as the child develops. When a parent or coach completes a lesson with the child, the tennis lesson needs to end when the child walks off the court. Let the child be a kid at home and have a normal life without the parent having the child read tennis articles or practice her forehand against the garage door. If the child chooses to continue tennis activities at home, let that be her decision and not yours.

The Coach's Role

The coach plays a key role in the tennis development of a child. Most of the time, the coach will serve as a role model and often a friend. The coach will be responsible for teaching the player mechanics, strategies, mental game, and his approach to the game. When I was growing up, my coach was a role model for me and was someone I looked up to very much. I will never forget him or the other coaches I worked with throughout my junior and college days. Children will remember their coaches probably the rest of their lives.

Carol L. Otis, M.D. in a recent USTA High-Performance Coaching Newsletter said, "The coach who has an understanding of the changes associated with physical, emotional and mental growth will be better equipped to communicate with the players and help them deal with any challenges that may arise along the way."

Below are some fundamentals to good coaching:

- Emphasize sportsmanship first and winning second
- Help set realistic goals for the student
- Understand you are a role model on and off the court. While watching the news with my parents one evening, we saw one of my former coaches busted for drugs. I looked up to this individual quite a bit, as I admired him as a coach and a friend. I now remember him as getting caught with drugs rather than the positives aspects in our coach student relationship.
- Know the latest teaching methods. Stay current and accept changes in the game.
- Be a leader, but not a dictator
- Make the experience working with the child one she will remember, rather than one she would soon forget.
- Communicate. Make sure you listen and don't dominate the conversation.
- Try to always find something positive in the lesson. End the lesson on a positive note.
- Dress professionally. Always come to the lesson dressed like a professional.
- Always be upbeat, ready to give 100% of your effort to your student.
- Emphasize fun!

When is My Child Ready for Tournaments?

To play in a beginner tournament, the child needs to be able to serve with occasional double faults, be able to establish a rally, and keep score. The decision whether the child is ready to play in a tournament should be a team effort. First of all, does the child want to play tournaments? The parent and coach might feel the player is ready to compete, but she might have no desire to play any type of match, let alone tournament play. If the player is ready to compete and shows the desire, the parent and coach need to discuss what type of tournament the player should play in. The coach should be knowledgeable in this area to insure the player is playing the type of competition she needs to compete against. We do not want the child to go play a high level sectional tournament when she should be playing a novice tournament. As a result, she may lose confidence in herself.

A few observations should help you determine if a player is ready for tournament play:

- Does the player desire competition? If the player is not showing signs wishing to compete, hold back until she comes to you desiring to play a tournament. Throwing her into the fire too early could result in the player developing frustration.
- Is the player mentally ready? She might wish to play tournaments, but will she be able to handle getting beat? Some children have a hard time handling defeat and it takes maturity to get through it. Practice matches are best until the coach believes she is ready for tournaments.

- Is the player physically ready? This is where the coach will be able to tell if she has strong enough mechanics necessary to compete in tournaments. What to look for:
  - o Footwork–can the player move to the ball, set her feet, and hit the ball under control?
  - o Ground strokes–is the player able to be reasonably consistent? She does not have to make 20 balls in a row, but needs to be able to sustain a rally.
  - o Serving consistently–everyone double faults. The child needs to be able to limit her double faults where they are not double faulting a game away.

Some children want to know when they get to play a tournament after their first day of holding a racket. This type of player can get their tournament-fix by playing competition drills and games located in this book. Another great program is USTA Jr. Team Tennis. You can get more information about it at www.usta.com.

Communication

Communication between the coach, parent, and child must be clear. A parent-player conference is always a good idea whether you meet with them once a year or more often. The coach needs to educate the child and parents on certain areas the player needs to work on to get to the next level, and let them know what "homework assignments" she needs to complete in order to solve those issues.

Also, the coach needs to inform the parent and child what junior programs she needs to sign up for: group drills, team tennis, or private lessons. A coach also needs to sit down and discuss his concerns with the parents if they are having discipline problems with the child.

A parent needs to feel free to speak with the child's coach and talk about the child's progress. Open communication with the parent and coach is vital for the success of the relationship and the tennis development of the child. The parent has a right to speak with the coach to discuss the player's progress. Do not speak with the coach during your child's private lesson. This is the time for the pro to coach and communicate with the child, and stepping in to speak with the pro interrupts the lesson, which usually results in the child losing focus. Set up a time to meet with the coach or speak with him after the lesson.

The best thing a parent can provide for the team is a positive environment. This environment consists of the coach and the parent being positive role models. Children look up to adults and people they care about. Make sure you and the coach are speaking and acting in a way which models good sportsmanship.

7
Easy as 1-2-3
Progressive Lesson Plans

Children from ages five to ten are such a joy to teach! Their looks of joy and expressions of excitement when they get praise for hitting successful backhands or simply bumping the balls on their rackets are just priceless. Moments like these make teaching children so much fun.

Children will respond well to the equipment just like they respond well to the equipment on a playground. They like using targets and props to aid them in their development. Remember to wear your funny hat!

Equipment Needed for Lesson Plans

1. Funny hat
2. Beanbags
3. Foam ball
4. Beach ball
5. Pee wee trainer
6. Cones
7. Low-compression balls
8. Field goal
9. Hula hoops
10. Ball hoppers
11. Clown nose
12. Teach feet
13. Flat targets
14. Fishing pole
15. Racket net

Progression

You will find different motor skills games or activities in each day of progressions. Motor skills are a very important part of this age group's development. Each drill has a time allotment to help you complete the session on time. However, use your judgment to expand the time on motor skill games if you feel the players need extra time. Do not feel as though you need to rush through each and every drill to complete it on time. We want to make sure the players in this age group are developing their motor skills properly.

Groundstrokes and serves are to be taught on the baseline of a 36' court for ages 5–7 and a 60' court for ages 8–10. Starting young players on the baseline of a 78' regulation court will frustrate most children. Most beginner players lack the strength and timing to hit a ball successfully from the baseline. They will be challenged sufficiently by being on the shorter tennis court. If you find that you need to shorten the court even more during your lessons, do so. I move my player up as close as I need to for him to experience early success. It's a good idea to invest in a 2′ 9″ tennis net for use with the lesson plans for 5–7-year olds. But if you do not have a shorter net, the standard 3′ net will be fine, or you can use yellow caution tape for the net until you purchase one. Just remember, use the short court.

Focus your training with the QuickStart format. This also goes for coaches and parents who are currently teaching 10-and-under players at the baseline of a 78′ court. The USTA will be implementing the QuickStart

format in USTA Jr. Team Tennis as well as USTA tournaments. If you do not have short court equipment, make sure you move the players up closer to the net, either at the service line area or "no-man's land" when teaching groundstrokes and serves. If you teach on a 78′ court, you can the use tape for lines and make a 36′ and 60′ court.

For the first four days of the session, feed balls on the same side of the court as the children. Simply toss the ball in front of them. You will have more control tossing a ball than you would feeding with your racket. By Day 5, you can move to the other side of the net. However, a particular group of players may not always be ready for this challenge. They need to develop their hand-eye coordination, so toss on the same side as the players as long as they need the practice.

On Day 10 for ages 5–7 and Day 9 for ages 8–10, players begin to play points. You need to emphasize getting the ball back in play rather than focusing too much on the mechanics. Bumping the ball back in play is a success and should be rewarded with many "high fives!" Players get bored and frustrated with tennis if the focus is always surrounded around mechanics. Get excited when the player makes the ball over the net and in the court!

On Day 12, players are introduced to the full motion serve. Prior to this development, players are taught to simply put their racket on their shoulder and make solid contact at full extension. Keep an eye on your students, especially the 5–7-year-olds, to make sure they are ready for the full motion serve. The serve can be challenging even while simplifying the mechanics, so make sure you are patient and understand they will not be hitting the serve like a pro after this session.

Make it Fun!
You cannot give too many "high-fives!"

Do you realize that these children will remember you as the one who introduced tennis to them? First impressions are so important to this age group. Make sure you come to work with a smile and an upbeat personality. You cannot give too many "high-fives!" Even if you are teaching a player who lacks in athletic ability, praise that individual when he makes contact with the ball. You might also come across a child who is continually disruptive in class. Take a deep breath and just remember you do not know what is going on in his personal life. Your class could be one of the few positive things going on at this time for him.

Make sure you have plenty of prizes to hand out through the day and make sure you do not leave anyone out. We do not want a child with hurt feelings because everyone in his group won a prize except for him. Also, the use of a skills chart (See sample skills chart on the following pages) can add excitement for the children. You can make a chart that fits what you are trying to accomplish for that particular week. For example, you might have a 5-point club for the forehand groundstroke. The child will be able to put a sticker in that box if he made 5 forehands in a row. After teaching the child, let him put a sticker on the chart on what he accomplished for that day. Make sure every child gets to put a sticker on the chart. To insure every child can put a sticker on the chart, you can have a column for best attitude, best hustle, or most improved. We don't want a child left out while he has to watch all of his friends get stickers. We want the kids to go home to their parents excited about what they learned and won in tennis class!

Progression Plan

Day	Ages 5-7	Ages 8-10
1	• Introduction of motor skill development • Stationary forehand groundstroke development	• Introduction of motor skill development • Stationary forehand groundstroke development
2	Stationary backhand groundstroke development	Stationary backhand groundstroke development
3	Introduction of volley	Introduction of volley
4	Introduction of serve: instructor toss	• Introduction of serve: instructor toss • Introduction of overheads
5	Groundstroke development: instructor moves back and tosses 12 feet from player	• Groundstroke development: instructor tosses from other side of net • Groundstroke footwork introduction: player begins to learn to move to the ball, set his feet and make contact with the ball
6	Continue volley development	Volley development: player moves to the ball and hits a volley
7	Continue serving development Introduction of overheads	• Continue serving development: introduction of the ball toss • Continue overhead development: instructor moves back when feeding
8	Continue groundstroke development: player begins to learn to move to the ball, set his feet and make contact with the ball	Footwork development
9	• Groundstroke development: instructor feeds on other side of net continuing to challenge players tracking the ball • Introduction of live ball rallies	Introduction of point play
10	Introduction of point play	Drills and games will continue to challenge this age group's footwork
11	• Introduction of keeping score • Continue serving development: introduction of the ball toss	• Introduction of keeping score • Continue point play development
12	Point play development	Introduction of the full motion serve
13	Groundstroke and point play development	Groundstroke, volley, and point play development
14	Groundstroke and volley development	Groundstroke, volley, and point play development
15	Introduction of the full motion serve	Serves, groundstroke, and point play development

Tasty Wrap-up Questions

Questions	Answers
Can you name the four grand slam tournaments?	Australian Open, French Open, Wimbledon, US Open
Can you name one professional tournament other than a grand slam tournament?	Indian Wells or any tournament that is playing during the time of instruction
Can you name two professional tennis players?	Henin Hardan, Roger Federer, Rafael Nadal, Venus Williams, Serena Williams, or any current or former ATP/WTA player
Can you name all the instructors?	The teaching staff
Can you demonstrate the stroke of the day?	Have the player show the rest of the players how to hit the stroke she learned today.
How long is a regulation tennis court?	78 feet
How wide is a regulation tennis court?	36 feet
How tall is the net at the center?	3 feet
Can you name the lines on the court?	Baseline, single sideline, double sideline, center mark, service line, center service line, double allies, and service boxes
Can you name the different parts of the racket?	Head, throat, handle, and strings
How many balls come in a can?	3 or 4
How many chances do you get to serve?	2 (Don't worry about lets)
What are the scores of a tennis game?	Love, 15, 30, 40, deuce, ad, game
What does *love* mean in tennis?	Zero points
What does USTA stand for?	United States Tennis Association

Example of a Skills Chart

Player	Forehand Groundstroke 5-point club	Forehand Groundstroke 10-point club	Backhand Groundstroke 5-point club	Backhand Groundstroke 10-point club	Volley 5-point club	Volley 10-point club	Serves 5-point club	Serves 10-point club	Hustle	Attendance
David										
Lisa										
Aspen										
Chloe										
Marc										
Ryan										

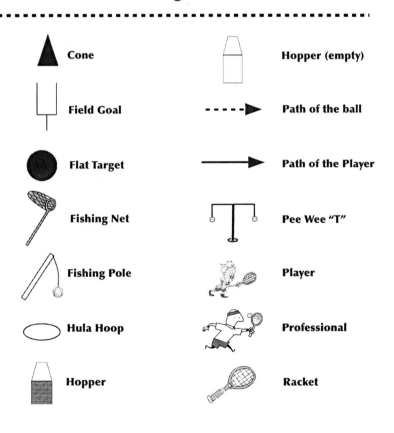

Singles Side Line		Doubles Alley	
Center Mark	Center	Deuce Box	
Baseline · Service Line	Service Line	Ad Box	
		Doubles Alley	

Doubles Side Line

Legend

Cone	Hopper (empty)
Field Goal	Path of the ball
Flat Target	Path of the Player
Fishing Net	Pee Wee "T"
Fishing Pole	Player
Hula Hoop	Professional
Hopper	Racket

Easy as 1-2-3 Lesson Plans for Ages 5–7

Day 1 – Stroke of the Day:
Introduction of Forehand Groundstroke

Equipment Needed: Funny hat, beanbag, foam ball, beach ball, pee wee trainer, and cones

1. Welcome/Take roll .... 3 minutes
2. Train - Warm up Learning the Lines .... 5 minutes

> **NOTE:**
> If you have purchased a 2′ 9″ net, bring it out for the ages 5–7 lesson plans. However, if you do not have one, no worries, the 3′ net will be fine until you purchase one or you can use yellow caution tape. Just make sure you shorten the tennis court.

> **NOTE:**
> I recommend using foam balls for ages 5–7. USTA also uses foam balls for the QuickStart format for ages 8 and under. However, if you live in a windy city such as I do, low-compression balls seem to do better in the wind.

Put on a funny hat and wear it throughout the day. The kids will laugh at the hat and begin to loosen up. Have students form a line behind you. Have the children follow you around all the lines on the court. While outlining all the lines, tell the players what the lines are. This is a good way to teach the lines of the court. You can change it up by doing the following:

A. Jog   D. Crawl like a bear
B. Bunny hop   E. Flap your wings like a bird
C. Skip

3. Safety Position and Grip .... 5 minutes

Safety position – players hug their racket pressing the racket against their chest. This is probably the most important lesson of the day. Teach the players to hug their rackets. When they stand in line, they need to have the racket in safety position so they won't accidentally hit someone. There are two ways that seem to work best in teaching an eastern grip to this age group:

A. Belly Button Grip – The player puts the butt of the grip to his belly button with the racket head straight up and down where he can't see the strings. Then he puts his hand flat on the strings and slides the hand down to the grip.

B. Shake Hands Grip – Shake hands with the player and then take his racket having the butt of the racket facing the player and the head at the angle where you cannot see the strings. Now have the player shake hands with the racket.

4. Racket Control.. 5 minutes

Players take a foam ball or beach ball and balance it on their rackets. Divide the players into two or three lines and do relays to keep them entertained during this important motor skill drill.

5. **Stroke of the Day: Forehand Groundstroke**................. 5 minutes

Spread the players out on the service line. Remember, players should have their rackets in safety position! This is now the time to teach them the forehand groundstroke by using the Easy as 1-2-3 short and sweet or loopy loop method. The players mirror you as you are swinging from position 1 to position 3.

6. **Forehands with the Trainer**.. 10 minutes

Set up a pee wee trainer with two dangling balls (see diagram). Have the players turn their sides, rackets in position 1 and swing through to position 3. After contact, player catches the ball and hits again. Challenge the players by having them hit a ball swung by the instructor or parent. Make sure the players are praised for making contact and swinging through to position 3.

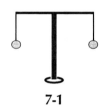

7-1
Pee Wee Trainer

7. **Forehands with a Bounce**... 5-10 minutes

Line the players up forming one line on the baseline of a 36' or 60' court. Using foam balls, drop the ball in front of the student allowing the player to make contact in front.

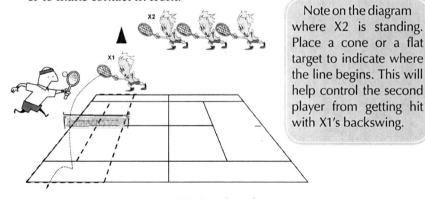

Note on the diagram where X2 is standing. Place a cone or a flat target to indicate where the line begins. This will help control the second player from getting hit with X1's backswing.

7-2 Forehands

REMINDER:

If you do not have lines for the 36' court or a 2'9" net, the regular service line on a 78' court will be fine, however the use of tape for the lines and yellow caution tape for the net will work for the 36' court.

9.   **Line Game** ....**5 minutes**

Review the lines on the court. Players line up at the fence. Yell out a line. The players then run to the line. If a player goes to the wrong line, he is out. As they get to know the lines better, increase the difficulty of the game by eliminating the last player to get to the line.

10. **Wrap up - Give out Prizes** ....**5 minutes**

Ask questions of the players for prizes such as, What was the stroke of the day? Can someone show us how to hold a forehand grip? Can you name one Grand Slam Tennis Tournament?

Day 2 – Stroke of the Day: Introduction of Backhand Groundstroke

Equipment Needed: Foam ball, pee wee trainer, field goal, and cones

1.   **Welcome/Take roll** ....**3 minutes**

2.   **Train** ....**5 minutes**

Children form a line behind you and follow you around all the lines on the court. While outlining all the lines, review the lines on the court.

3.   **Review Forehand – Field Goal!** ....**10 minutes**

Set up a field goal at the net. Bounce a foam ball in front of the player having him hit a forehand from Position 1 to Position 3 in between the poles for a field goal! Bounce three balls to each player and rotate. Have them keep their own score. Player scores one point for each field goal made. First player to ten wins!

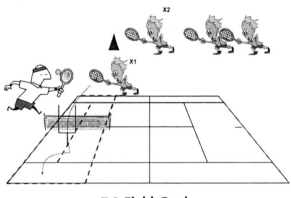

7-3 Field Goal

4.   **Stroke of the Day: Backhand Groundstroke** ....**5 minutes**

At this age, keep the grip simple by using the Eastern-Eastern grip. Don't make it complicated by changing the right hand (for a right-handed player) for a two-handed backhand. As they progress and get into private lessons, you will know when it is time to change their grip. At this time the player needs to enjoy early success by making contact and not having to worry about grip changes. You will find a lot of players change to their right hand naturally.

Spread the players out on the service line. Remember, players should have their rackets in safety position! Teach the backhand groundstroke by using the Easy as 1-2-3 method. Have the players mirror you as you are swinging through from position 1 to position 3.

5. **Backhands with the Rope** .... 10 minutes
Set up a pee wee trainer with two dangling balls. Have the players turn their sides, put their rackets in position 1 and swing through to position 3. After contact, players catch the ball and hit again. Increase the difficulty by having the players hit balls swung by the pro. Make sure the players are praised for making contact and swinging through to position 3. You can never give enough "high-fives!"

7-4 Pee Wee Trainer

6. **Sandwich Relays** .... 5 minutes
Take a break from backhands for a few minutes and play Sandwich Relays. Divide the players into two lines. Two players from each team sandwich a ball in between their rackets and race to the cone and back.

7. **Backhands with a Bounce** .... 10 minutes
Form the players into one line at the baseline of a 36' court. Using foam balls, drop the ball in front of the student allowing the player to make contact in front. Note on the diagram where X2 is standing, place a cone or a flat target to indicate where the line begins. This will help control the second player from getting hit with X1's backswing.

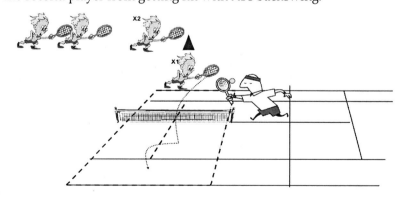

7-5 Backhands with a Bounce

8. **Simon Says**..5 minutes

This is a fun game that you can use to review what they have learned the past few days. The following are a few examples for Simon to say or not to say:

A. Touch your shoulders
B. Touch your hips
C. Forehand position 1
D. Backhand position 1
E. Backhand position 2

9. **Wrap up**..3-5 minutes

Ask questions of the players for prizes such as, *What was the stroke of the Day? Can you name all the instructors? What stroke did you learn yesterday?*

Day 3 – Stroke of the Day: Introduction of Volley

Equipment Needed: Foam balls, hula hoop, pee wee trainer, cones, hoppers, and a clown nose.

1. **Welcome/Take roll**..3 minutes

2. **Warm up with a Relay**..5 minutes

Divide players into two teams. Put out two empty hoppers at the net and one hopper full of balls at the center mark. Each player takes a ball from the full hopper and balances the ball on his racket with his palm up and places the ball into the empty hopper at the net. Then he runs back to his line and tags the next player. After the relay is completed, play it again, but with the palm facing down.

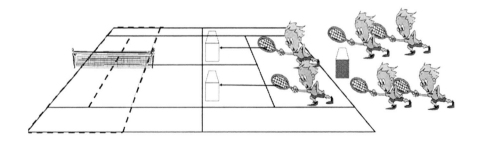

7-6 Warm up with a Relay

3. Review Forehand/Backhand Groundstrokes -
    Tennis Baseball...10 minutes

    Make sure players are lined up on the baseline of the 36' court. Contin-
    ue to feed balls from the same side as player. In the first game, play with
    instructor tossing foam balls to forehands. X1 hits a forehand. If the ball
    lands anywhere in the singles court, the player will remain "safe" and
    then goes to the end of the line. If he makes an error, he is "out" and
    has to run around to the other side of the net while dropping his racket
    off the court. The person who is "out" now tries to catch someone else's
    shot. If he catches the ball, he returns to the "batting side" and replaces
    the player who hit the ball. Eventually only one player is left batting
    and the rest of the players are trying to catch the shot. If the last player
    hits the ball in without the ball getting caught, he wins the game. If the
    last player misses the shot, he is now "out" and all the other players
    are now "safe." Change to backhands in the second game and alternate
    forehands/backhands in the third game.

> **NOTE:**
> You will find that foam balls are sometimes hard to catch. The use of low-
> compression balls will be fine to use in Tennis Baseball.

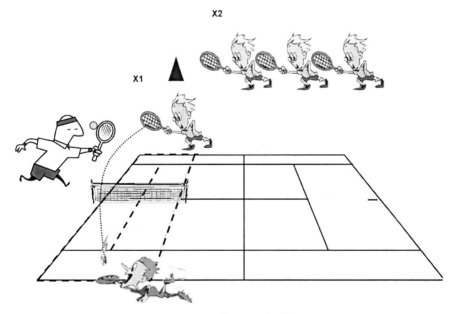

7-7 Tennis Baseball

4. **Stroke of the Day – Volleys** .... 5 minutes

    Spread the players along the net. Keep the grip simple and have the players use the same Eastern grip as forehand groundstroke. Have the player use two hands for the backhand volley for support. Make it as simple as possible for this age group.

    Demonstrate how to hit a forehand and backhand volley as they mirror you. On the backhand volley have the players use two hands for stability. Remember, punch, don't swing!

5. **Volley** .... 10 minutes

    Using the pee wee trainer, the instructor swings the ball softly to the player's forehand volley. Make sure the player has his side turned with the racket in front of his body. Do not start him in Ready Position (Ready Position, Turn, and Step will be discussed on Day 6). After two or three rotations, switch to the backhand volley.

6. **Hit My Nose!** .... 10 minutes

    Wear a Clown Nose. Using foam balls, toss a ball to the player and have him hit a forehand volley trying to hit your clown nose. Set out teach feet to help players know where to step. After two or three rotations, switch to backhand volleys.

7. **Volley Basketball** .... 10 minutes

    Lay out a hula hoop. Using the forehand volley, a player hits a foam ball fed by the instructor into the hula hoop. Feed three consecutive balls to a player. Players rotate. Have the players keep track of how many "baskets" they make. Each shot in the hula hoop scores one point. First player to 10 wins! If players are struggling to make it into the hula hoop, set up one or two additional hula hoops. Switch to the backhand volley after five minutes of forehand volleys.

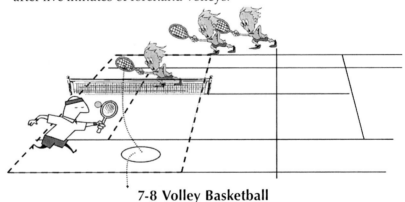

7-8 Volley Basketball

8. Wrap up with the Line Game .... 5 minutes

Day 4 – Stroke of the Day: Introduction of Serve

Equipment Needed: Funny hat, beanbags, foam balls, low-compression balls, teach feet, fishing pole, and field goal

1. **Welcome/Take roll**..3 minutes
Instructor wears a funny hat today.

2. **Simon Says**..5 minutes

3. **Beanbag Toss**..5 minutes
Working on hand eye-coordination, half of the group spreads out on the single sideline and the other half spreads out on the doubles sideline. Each player needs to be directly across from another player. Each player tosses a beanbag with their racket to the other player directly across from them. The player across the alley catches the beanbag with his racket. Tell the players they are tossing the beanbag over a river.

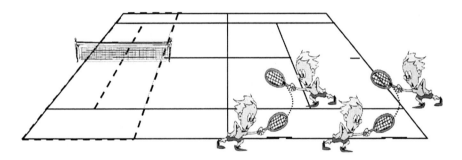

7-9 Beanbag Toss

4. **Stroke of the Day: Serve**..3 minutes
Line the players along the service line or the baseline of the 36' court. Teach them the difference between the Deuce and Ad box and where they should stand when hitting a serve. Have the players mirror you as you explain how to hit a serve. At this point in their development, the players should start with the rackets on their shoulders. It is not necessary to teach them the entire motion from starting position to the back scratch position. Remember, we want the players to have early success and starting with the rackets on their shoulders will speed up the success. Players should keep the Eastern grip. The palm should be up with the racket face open so the player can put a drink on the racket like a waiter. Remember, keep it simple and don't have a lot of grip changes. Emphasize reaching to full extension and hitting up on the ball.

5. **Hitting Serves with the Fishing Pole** .... 10-15 minutes

    The fishing pole is a great tool to teach students to reach up on the serve and to make solid contact without the difficulty of throwing the ball toss in the proper spot. Have the players form a line and let the players hit from the fishing pole three times and then rotate. Use teach feet to insure their feet are positioned properly. Make it fun and help them hit up on the ball by doing the following variations:

    A. Have the players get on their knees and hit the ball off the fishing pole.

    B. Have the players get on their backs and hit the ball off the fishing pole.

6. **Serves with the Instructor's Toss** .... 10 minutes

    Form a line at the baseline of a 36' court. Move the player towards the net if this will help him with early success. Do not have this age group begin at the baseline of a 78' regulation court to hit serves. The first player comes up with his racket on his shoulder. Have the player step on the teach feet. Throw up the ball toss with a foam ball or low-compression ball. When the player is hitting the serve, his goals are to make solid contact and to have the ball clear the net. These are direct results from the training in Drill 5. Make this drill fun by keeping score. Each student scores one point if he hits the ball over the net and he scores two points if he hits the ball in the proper service box. First player to seven points wins a prize!

7. **Groundstroke Development – Field Goal** .... 10 minutes

    Make this drill fun by setting up the field goal and having them hit through it for points. With foam balls or low-compression balls have each player hit four balls, alternating forehands and backhands. Feed balls from same side as player.

8. **Wrap up** .... 5-10 minutes

    Give out prizes to all the players for their great efforts throughout the session. Stickers, candy, and certificates are some ideas for prizes.

Day 5 - Stroke of the Day:
Groundstroke Development

Equipment Needed: Beanbags, funny hat, and foam balls

1. Welcome/Take Roll...3 minutes

2. Train - Warm up Learning the Lines ....5 minutes
   Instructor puts on a funny hat. Children form a line behind you and
   follow you around all the lines on the court. While outlining all the
   lines, review the lines on the court. You can change it up by doing the
   following:
   A. Jog
   B. Bunny hop
   C. Skip

3. Alley Rally! ....5-10 minutes
   This drill works on motor skills and warms up players with the rackets
   in their hands. Half the players line up on the singles sideline and the
   other half line up along the doubles sideline, with the players from each
   line facing each other. Place a ball just to the right (if he is right-handed)
   of the player about two feet in front of him. This will serve as the target
   for the player across from him. With the rackets in their hands (palm
   up) they now bump the ball to each other trying to hit the ball in front of
   the player across them. Players must let the ball bounce to bump the ball
   back. If player hits the target (ball across from him), he gets one point.

7-10 Alley Rally

4. Groundstrokes - The 10-Point Club...............................10 minutes
   Players form a line at the baseline of a 36′ court. Continue to feed on the
   same side as the player but move back approximately 12 feet from the

player. With foam balls, feed four balls alternating to his forehand and backhand. Make it fun for the players by adding a point to their totals every time they make a shot. Their goal is to get enough points to join the 5-point club and then the 10-point club and so on.

5.   **Hit My Funny Hat** .... 10 minutes
This drill challenges the players' groundstrokes. Stand on the other side of the net of the players and toss foam balls. Have them try to hit the funny hat on your head. Help them with the timing by saying, "bounce...hit." Have them say it with you. Go five minutes on the forehand and five minutes on the backhand.

6.   **Tennis Baseball** .... 10 minutes
Feed approximately twelve feet from player. Alternate feeds to the forehand and backhand.

7.   **Don't Let the Egg Drop!** .... 10 minutes
Divide into two groups. X1 and X2 run to the net. As they are running, they are rolling the ball on each other's racket back and forth. This drill continues to work on their motor skills as they have to concentrate on not dropping the ball off the racket as they are rolling it to their partner's racket on the move.

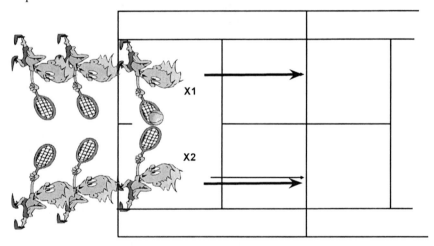

7-11 Don't Let the Egg Drop

8.   **Wrap up – Give out Prizes** .... 5 minutes
Ask questions of the players for prizes such as, *What is the most important stroke in the game of tennis? What is this line called?* (Point to a particular line on the court.) *Who just won the US Open?* (Ask about any major tennis tournament that just completed.)

Day 6 - Stroke of the Day:
Volley Development

Equipment Needed: Foam balls, racket net, teach feet, and a field goal

1. **Welcome/Take roll** .... **3 minutes**

2. **Clean Your Plate** .... **5 minutes**
   This popular drill is used for warming up players. Each player lays his racket down in a large circle with four balls on each racket. When the instructor says "Go!" each player takes one ball at a time off his racket and puts it on someone else's racket. They are trying to get their own racket (plate) empty. The first player to get an empty racket (plate) wins. This drill could go on for a while, so you might have to stop the drill once the players begin to tire.

3. **Review and Warm-up the volley** .... **10-15 minutes**
   Review how to hit the volley, emphasizing contact in front of their body, and to punch (not swing) at the ball. Divide the players into two lines, one line hitting forehand volleys and the other hitting backhand volleys. Use foam balls and teach feet to insure they are stepping properly. After the player has hit three volleys, have him go to the end of the other line. After you feel they are warmed up, proceed to challenge them by having them start in ready position, turn, and step. You can make this drill fun by playing "10-point club." As they get better, challenge the players by using smaller targets such as the service box or a hula hoop. At the end of the clinic, give each player who made it into the 10-point club a sticker.

4. **Bus Driver** .... **10 minutes**
   This is a very popular game with students but it is only as fun as the instructor makes it. Use foam balls for this game. Line the players along the net spacing them out where they can hit a volley without hitting another player. The object is to end up as the bus driver (X1) after a pre-determined time (i.e. five minutes). The instructor tosses a ball to any player. If the player misses, he moves to the end of the bus and everyone else advances. Make this game fun and exciting. Looking one way and tossing the other will keep everyone on their toes! After the time is up, whoever is the bus driver is the winner!

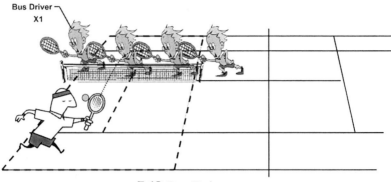

7-12 Bus Driver

5. **Hockey Tennis**..**10-15 minutes**
    Divide players into two teams. Set up a field goal approximately twelve
    feet behind the net and use foam balls. X2 plays the goalie using the
    racket net. Instructor feeds to X1. X1 is hitting a groundstroke trying
    to get the ball past the goalie through the field goal. If X2 catches the
    volley with the racket net, she scores one point for her team. If X1 hits it
    past the goalie and in the goal, he scores one points for his team. After
    game is over, have the teams switch sides.

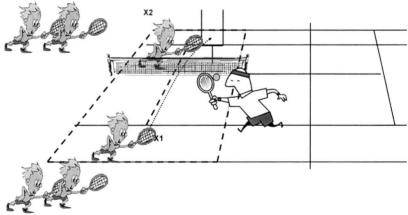

7-13 Hockey Tennis

6. **Simon Says Line Test**..**5-10 minutes**
    Play Simon Says by having the players walk or run to the lines on the
    court including the deuce and ad boxes. By now players should under-
    stand all the lines on the court. Challenge the players by having Simon
    say a line on the other side of the court.

7. **Wrap up and dismiss players**...**3 minutes**

Day 7 – Stroke of the Day:
Overheads and Serve Development

Equipment Needed: Foam balls, teach feet, flat targets, cones, and a fishing pole

1. Welcome/Take Roll...3 minutes

2. Red Light, Green Light...5-10 minutes

   This is a great Warm up game. Have the players line up at the fence while you're at the net. When you yell "Green Light!" the players walk as fast as they can until you yell "Red Light!" First player to the net wins! Variations include having them running, balancing a ball, bumping the ball down, or bumping the ball up.

3. Review Groundstrokes and Volleys.............................10 minutes

   Set up teach feet or flat targets to indicate where the players will run to hit their shots. Toss the balls to the players. Player will move and hit a forehand groundstroke and then proceed to the next spot to hit a forehand volley. After the volley, the player goes to the end of the line. After five minutes, change the drill to the backhand side. This is a simple Warm up drill and moves pretty fast so players don't have to wait in line long. Make sure when they get to the target they set their feet. This introduces players to more advanced concepts such as moving to the ball, setting their feet, and getting their body under control before hitting the shot. On Day 8, players will be challenged with tracking and prediction.

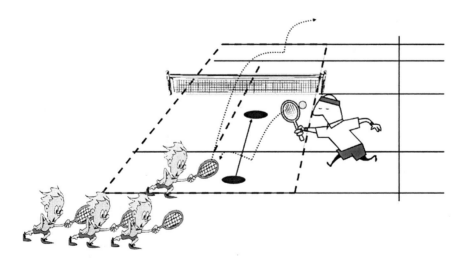

7-14 Review Groundstrokes

4. **Overheads with the Fishing Pole** .... 5-10 minutes

Hold the fishing pole in front of the student, designating where the ball would be for an overhead. Form a line and have the first player about three feet from the net hitting down on the ball. Make sure player starts with the racket back on the shoulder in the scratch back position. Players hit three balls from the fishing pole. This drill works on overheads, but it also works on serving mechanics. It teaches players to hit down and through the ball. Rotate five to seven times.

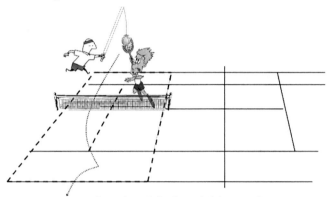

7-15 Overheads with the Fishing Pole

5. **Overheads with the Pro's Toss** .... 5-10 minutes

Form a line and have the first player about three feet from the net. Stand approximately three feet away from the net on the other side of the court and toss the foam ball up as the player hits down on the ball. This drill is challenging the player more by having them learn proper timing for contact. Help them by saying, "toss and hit" at the proper time. Make it fun by dividing the group into two teams. When a player makes the shot, he scores one point for his team. First team to fifteen wins.

6. **Review the Serve** .... 3 minutes

Review the mechanics of the serve. At this point, do not teach players the full motion of the serve. They are still trying to develop timing while reaching up and making solid contact. The racket should start back on the shoulder.

7. **Serves with the Pro's Toss** .... 5-10 minutes

Form a line and have the first player at the service line. The player steps on the teach feet. Toss up a foam ball. If you find the players having a hard time hitting the toss, pull out the fishing pole for a few rotations.

8. **Wrap up – Line Game** .... 3 minutes

Remember to ask them which box is the deuce and the ad box on both sides of the court.

Day 8 – Stroke of the Day: Footwork Development

Equipment Needed: Funny hat and foam balls

1. Welcome/Take Roll...3 minutes

2. Caterpillar...5-10 minutes

Wear a funny hat today. Divide the group into two equal teams. Line one team behind baseline parallel to single sideline. Do the same with the other team on the other single sideline of the same side of the court. Have all the players hold their rackets in front of them with their palms up. X1 will roll his ball on his neighbor's racket. After successfully passing the ball off, X1 will run behind his teammates to the beginning of the line. If a player drops the ball, the team has to start over. First team to the net wins!

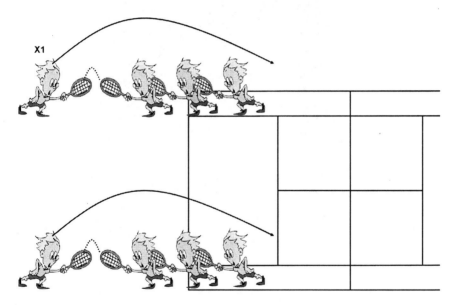

7-16 Caterpillar

3. **Balance the Racket!** ....5 minutes

This drill works on hand-eye coordination. Divide half of the players on the single sideline and the other half on the doubles sideline. Have the players face each other in pairs. Each player stands with the racket on the right side of his body, with the racket head touching the ground. Make sure all the players' rackets are lined up directly across from their partners' rackets. When the instructor says "Go!" the players let go of their rackets and run across the alley to catch their partners' rackets before they hit the ground. If both partners catch the rackets before they hit the ground, that pairing receives one point. First pair to get to five points wins!

7-17 Balance the Racket

SAFETY NOTE: Make sure the players are not lined up across from each other. You don't want the players to run into each other. They should be at an angle as indicated in the diagram.

4.   Hit Recover..10 minutes
Continuing to challenge the players' groundstrokes, this game teaches them how to move to the ball, set their feet, and hit the groundstroke. Feed from the other side of the net. Make sure you emphasize the child setting his feet. At this point, I would hope the player naturally loads up in an open stance forehand, but if not, no worries. If the player hits from a square or closed stance, that is fine as long as he is balanced. Have the player move from point A to point B, hit a forehand, and then recover back to A. Player hits three low-compression balls and goes to the end of the line. Hit five minutes of forehands and then rotate to backhands. Make it fun for the players by doing the 10-point club game.

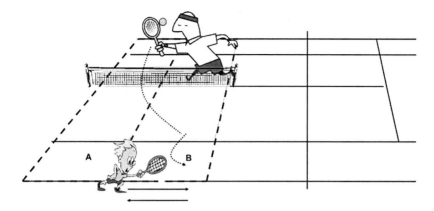

7-18 Hit Recover

5. **Groundstroke – Volley** .... 10 minutes

This drill continues to develop footwork. Have the player move from A to B and hit a forehand groundstroke using foam balls, then move from B to C and hit a forehand volley. This is a great time to teach the players the "split step." Go five minutes on the forehand side and then switch to the backhand side. Make it fun, let them play to the 10-point club. Make sure you give the players a prize if they make it into the club!

> The split step is part of the transition from the baseline to the net. The player generates a short and quick hop to control his body as his weight is evenly distributed on the balls of his feet.

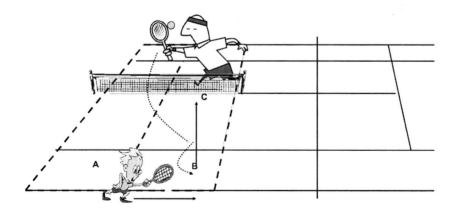

7-19 Groundstroke – Volley

6. **Tennis Baseball with Footwork**..................................... 10 minutes

   Play Tennis Baseball tossing the ball out and away from the player, forcing him to move to his right, set his feet, pivot, and hit through the ball all the way to position 3. Feed to the backhand for the second game. For the third game alternate feeds to the forehand and backhand.

7. **Side to Side - Hit My Funny Hat** .... 10 minutes

   Feed each player four foam balls and then rotate. Alternate feeds to the forehand and then the backhand. The players are trying to hit your funny hat. If they hit it, they get a prize!

8. **Wrap up**.. 5-10 minutes

   Hand out prizes to all the players for their efforts throughout the session. If you use a Skills Chart, this is a great time to have the students put the stickers on the board. Make it visible so the parents can see. It will get the players excited to have their parents watch them put a sticker on the Skills Chart.

Day 9 – Stroke of the Day: Groundstroke Development

Equipment Needed: Funny hat, ball hopper, low-compression balls or foam balls, and hula hoops

1. **Welcome/Take Roll**... 3 minutes

   OPTIONAL: You can now begin the use of low-compression balls if you wish. According to USTA, the QuickStart format with a 36′ court uses foam balls. As the player progresses, and you decide to move the player to a 60′ court, use low-compression balls. My advice is to keep using foam balls unless the player exhibits very good athleticism and exceptional tracking and prediction, along with the ability to control his body when moving and hitting the ball.

2. **Ball Relay – Pro Wears a Funny Hat Today**............... 5-10 minutes

   Place three rackets along single sideline and three more along opposite single sideline on same side of the court. Form two teams. The first player takes a ball out of the hopper (located at the center mark) and runs to put the ball on the first racket and then runs back to the hopper and gets another ball. He runs to the second racket and places the ball on the racket and runs back to retrieve a third ball from the hopper. He runs to the third racket, places the ball on the racket and runs back to the line to tag the next player in line. The next player in line runs to the first racket and takes the ball off and puts it back into the hopper. She does this for the second and third racket. The drill goes on until a team completes the drill first and is declared the winner!

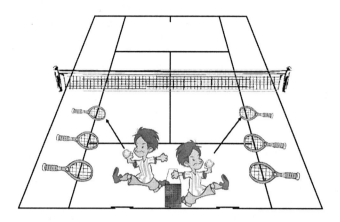

7-20 Ball Relay

3. **Aerobic Drill with a Toss**.. **10 minutes**
    Toss the ball from the other side of the net. This drill continues to challenge the players by having them move and hit the shot, rather than the previous stationary drills. This is a fast drill where the player hits two balls and goes to the end of the line. X1 hits backhand and then slides over to hit a forehand. The player then goes to the end of the line. All players are hitting from the baseline of a 36′ court.

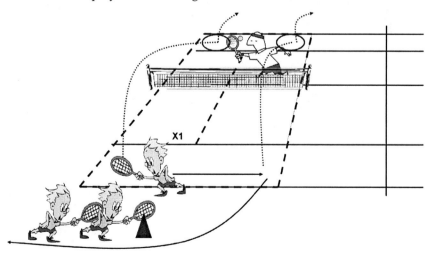

7-21 Aerobic Drill

4. **Side-to-Side - Hit My Funny Hat** .... **10 minutes**

    Feed each player four balls and then rotate. Make sure the players are moving to the shot. Emphasize getting their feet set and then hitting the ball. Alternate feeds to the forehand and backhand. The players are trying to hit your funny hat. If they hit it, they get a prize!

5. **Rally! Rally!** .... **15 minutes**

    For this age group, divide the court into two or four 36' x 18' courts depending on how many players you have. Have the players drop and hit and learn how to keep a rally going! If the player struggles with his drop and hit, feed the ball to him.

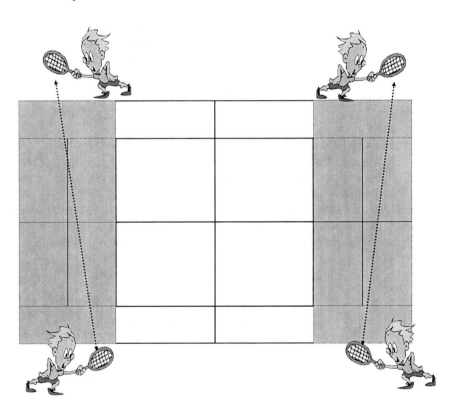

7-22 Rally Rally

6. **Line Game** .... **5 minutes**

    Review the lines on the court with the players.

Day 10 – Stroke of the Day:
Volley and Groundstroke Development; Introduction of Point Play

Equipment Needed: Hula hoop, field goal, and low-compression balls or foam balls

1. **Welcome/Take Roll**..**3 minutes**

2. **Red light/Green light**...**5 minutes**
   Have the players line-up along the fence. When you say, "Green light!" players walk as fast as they can towards the net. When you say, "Red light!" they have to stop. The following are some ideas for this game:
   A. Balance a ball
   B. Bump up - palm up, next game palm down
   C. Bump down
   D. Roll the ball around their racket

3. **Volley Warm up** ....**10 minutes**
   Divide the players into two lines with the first two players of each line at the net. Make sure the second players in line are standing where they won't get hit by the players hitting the volleys. Make sure players are starting in ready position, pivoting, and hitting the volley. As players get better, you can stretch your feeds out a little wider, forcing the player to lunge a bit. X1 hits two forehand volleys aiming in the hula hoop. He then goes to the end of the backhand volley line. X2 does the same, only hitting backhand volleys.

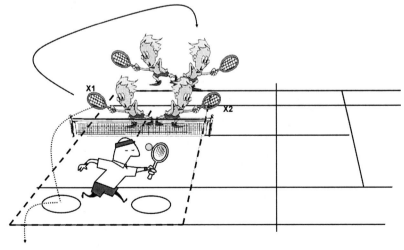

7-23 Volley

4. **Field Goal! - Side-to-Side Volleys** .... **10 minutes**

   This drill continues to work on the players' volley development while focusing on footwork. Have the players hit forehand and backhand volleys, alternating feeds to each side. Each player hits four balls trying to hit the ball through the field goal. Player then goes to the end of the line. Have them try to make the 10-point club or 20-point club, depending on how well they are progressing.

5. **Groundstroke-Volley Combination** .... **10 minutes**

   Continuing to challenge the players' groundstrokes and volleys with footwork, have the players line up at the baseline. X1 comes in and hits a forehand down the line. He then moves in, split steps, and hits a forehand volley. Make sure the player's body is under control while hitting the groundstroke and then the volley. Don't get too quick with the feeds. Make sure the players are set first. If the player makes both shots in zone A, he scores one point. First player to five wins! After five minutes, change drill to the backhand side.

7-25 Groundstroke-Volley Combination

6. **King of the Court – Point Play** .... **15 minutes**
   Players are introduced to singles play in this drill. Divide the players into two groups, half on the A side and the other half on the B side. The players on the B side feed the ball themselves. However, if the players have a hard time starting the point, you will need to feed the ball. The players can only score a point on the A side. If the player on the B side wins, the reward is to move to the A side where he can try to score points. If the player loses on the A side, he goes to the B side. First player to eleven wins!

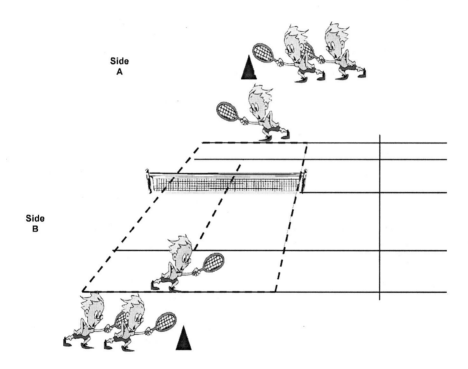

7-25 King of the Court

7. **Wrap up** .... **5 minutes**
   Ask questions for prizes. The questions should be focused around the day's highlights. Remind the players that tomorrow is Hat Day! Everyone wears a hat tomorrow.

Day 11 – Stroke of the Day: Introduction of the Service Ball Toss, Point Play Development, and Keeping Score

Equipment Needed: Beanbags, hula hoop, field goal, fishing pole, flat targets, and low-compression balls or foam balls. Today is Hat Day, and each player wears a hat.

1. Welcome/Take roll..3 minutes

2. Beanbag Toss ....5 minutes

    Begin by lining up half the players on the doubles sideline and the other half on the singles sideline. Have the players pair up and face their partners. Give each player on one side a beanbag. With their racket in hand, have the players toss the beanbag with their rackets to their partners. The other players catch the beanbag with their rackets. Go for one to two minutes at this distance and then have both lines take one big step back. Continue for one to two minutes. Then have the players take another step back and proceed for one to two minutes.

3. **Target Practice - Forehand/Backhand Groundstroke Review and Warm up**..10 minutes

    Set up the field goal and a hula hoop. Have the first player hit a forehand through the field goal and then slide over and hit a backhand into the hula hoop. If they make it in the field goal or in the hula hoop, they score two points for each shot made. They get one point if they make the shot in the court, but fail to make it through the field goal or in the hula hoop.

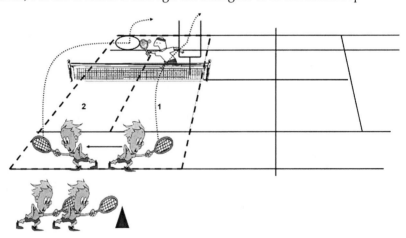

7-27 Target Practice

4. **Serve Warm up and Introduction of Ball Toss** .... **15 minutes**
Warm up by using the fishing pole. Each player hits three balls and rotates. This should take approximately five minutes.
Spread the players out along the service line and have them toss the ball trying to hit the target, which is placed at one o'clock. Do this for two-three minutes.
Divide the players into two lines and have one player from each line come up to to the baseline of a 36' court and hit two serves using their own ball toss.

5. **Introduction of Keeping Score** .... **10 minutes**
Teach the players how to keep score. Begin with love, 15, 30, 40, deuce, ad-in, ad-out, game. Your goal is for them to understand basic scoring by the end of the day. Don't overwhelm the players by getting into two out of three sets, tiebreakers, and match tiebreakers. At this age, it will be an accomplishment for them to learn to score a game. As they progress and continue in your program, begin to introduce sets and tiebreakers.
Form two teams. Players serve from the baseline of a 36' court. The first player from each team comes up and serves. One team serves into the deuce box and the other team into the ad box. If the player makes the serve (if the player misses, he gets a second serve), his team wins a point, resulting in the score being 15–love. If the player double faults, the score is love–15. The next player in line comes in to serve and the same rules apply. If the player makes it, the score would be 30-love. First team to "game" wins! After each game, switch sides. Play four times.

6. **Team Single Points** .... **15 minutes**
Divide into two teams. Use one 36' court if you have 5 or less players, or use two 36' courts if you have 6-8 players. Players feed their own ball to

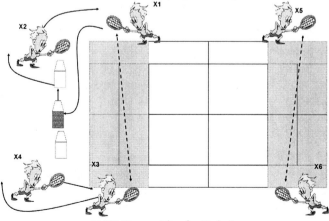

7-27 Team Single Points

begin the point. As seen on the diagram, the teams are divided by Team A on one side and Team B on the other side. Each court plays out 2 out of 3 points. The winning player, X1, runs to the hopper full of balls, grabs one ball, puts it into his team's hopper and then goes to the end of his team's line. The player who did not win, X3, goes to the end of this line. X1 is replaced by X2 and X3 is replaced by X4. The same format applies for players X5 and X6. Play two out of three 5-minute sets. After the five minutes are up, call time and count how many balls each team has in their hopper. Whoever has the most balls, wins that set. This game moves quickly and reduces standing in line for a long period of time.

7. **Tennis Baseball**.. **10 minutes**
Finish the day with the popular game, Tennis Baseball. Since this is Hat Day, let the players catch the ball with their hats. Make sure you challenge the players by making them move to hit the low-compression ball, rather than standing still for stationary feeds. The pro can make this drill entertaining by acting like they are going to feed to the forehand side but actually feed to the backhand. The players at this age respond well to this.

8. **Wrap up**... **5 minutes**
Ask questions for prizes. This is a great time to test what they learned about keeping score.

Day 12 – Stroke of the Day: Point Play Development

Equipment Needed: Low-compression balls or foam balls, funny hat, cones, and teach feet

1. **Welcome/Take Roll**... **3 minutes**

2. **Simon Says**... **5 minutes**
Wear a funny hat today. This game is a great review of the Easy as 1-2-3 method. It is also a great warm up when players are instructed to touch certain areas of their body quickly. For example: Simon says touch your toes, touch your shoulders, touch your hips, touch your ankles, etc, etc. Make sure you talk fast so they will get a good warm up!

3. **Racket Skills Relay** .... **5 minutes**
Divide players into two teams. Set out two cones, one for each line to run to. In game one, have the players bump the ball up as they run to the cone and back. In game two, have the players bump the ball up to the cone and back.

4. **Serves** .... 10 minutes

Players are working on the full service motion. Serve from the baseline of a 36′ court. Form two lines. Have two players come up to the baseline, one hitting to the deuce box and the other serving to the ad box. Each player gets two serves and then switches lines. Use teach feet to help the player to know where to stand.

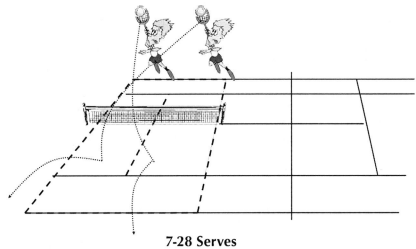

7-28 Serves

5. **Rally Ball** .... 15 minutes

Divide into two teams and separate teams on each side of the court. Have two players from each team stand on the baseline of a 36′ court. Feed the ball to X1. X1 hits the ball and plays out a doubles point. If X1

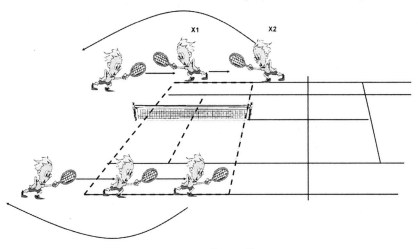

7-27 Rally Ball

misses the feed, he gets a "second serve" (second feed). After rally is completed, both teams rotate. A new player comes in to take X1's spot and X1 moves to X2's spot and X2 goes to the end of the line. Teams are rewarded a point each time they make the ball in the court. The game emphasizes success on making a shot rather than winning a point. Have a parent or fellow instructor keep score. After everyone from a team receives a feed, feed to the other team and continue to rotate for ten minutes. Each set is timed ten minutes. Play two out of three sets.

6. **Team Around the World**...**15 minutes**

Divide the players into two equal teams. Separate the teams on each side of the court. After you feed a ball to X1, he hits the ball and runs to the end of the line. X2 returns X1's ball and then goes to the end of the line. X3 returns X2's shot and goes to the end of the line. This goes on until someone misses a shot. When a player misses the shot, he sits down and is out of the game. The game will end when there are no players left from one of the teams.

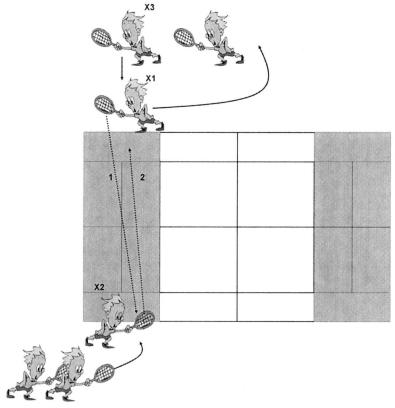

7-30 Team Around the World

7. Wrap up...5 minutes
Give everyone who participated in the program a prize. Ask questions for additional prizes. This is a great way to review everything the players learned throughout the program.

Day 13 – Stroke of the Day: Groundstroke Development and Point Play

Equipment Needed: Low-compression balls or foam balls and ball machine

1. Welcome/Take Roll...3 minutes

2. Line Game with Balance ....5 minutes
Work on the children's balancing skills while playing the line game. Call out a line and the players have to walk fast or run to the line while balancing the balls on their rackets. If a player drops a ball or he goes to the wrong line, he is out. Last player standing wins.

3. Groundstroke Relay..10 minutes
Divide the players into two teams and have them line up behind the baseline of a 36′ court. Feed the ball to the first player to reach the baseline and then feed to the other player. One team hits forehands and the other team hits backhands. The players hit the groundstroke and then tag the next player in line, regardless if they make the shot or not. After the game, have the team reverse sides. A variation to this game is not allowing the players to tag the next player in line until they make the shot. Another variation is the first team to make 10 shots, wins!

4. Team Groundstroke Points...10 minutes
Divide into two teams. One team hits forehands and the other team hits backhands. Each team is hitting down the line in between the single sideline and the center of the court. If the player makes the shot, he scores one point for the team. First team to ten wins. A variation to this game is setting out two field goals or two hula hoops. If the player makes it through the field goal or in the hula hoop, the player scores two points for the team.

5. Ball Machine Drill ....10 minutes
Set the ball machine on low speed simulating your feeds. Have the players hit three balls from the baseline of a 36′ court and then go to the end of the line. The Tennis Tutor Twist is a great machine that was specifically designed for this age group.

6. **Beat the Pro!**...**15 minutes**
   Form a line on one side of the net. One player comes up to the baseline
   of a 36′ court baseline and plays a point versus the instructor. Player
   only plays one point. Players will enjoy this game for the simple fact
   they are playing against their instructor. Make it fun, by making a "big
   deal" when a player beats you! If the player wins, he gets a prize.

7. **Wrap up** ....**5 minutes**
   Ask the players questions for prizes. Give the players a homework
   assignment to work on their bump ups and downs. There might be a
   test tomorrow!

Day 14 – Stroke of the Day: Volley and Groundstroke Development

Equipment Needed: Low-compression balls or foam balls, beanbags,
racket net, and hoppers

1. **Welcome/Take Roll**..**3 minutes**

2. **Bump Ups and Downs Test**...**10 minutes**
   Chart how many bump ups and downs the players can do in a row.
   Reward the player who gets the most for both with a prize. Recognize
   the players again at the end of the day.

3. **Beanbag Volleys**..**5 minutes**
   Divide the players into two lines. One line hits forehand volleys and the
   other line hits backhand volleys. Toss a beanbag to the player. Teach the
   players racket control and not to swing. The player catches the bag on
   his racket and then hand tosses it back to you. A variation of this game
   is to have the players pair up. Player 1 tosses the bean bag to player 2
   who catches it on his racket. He then tosses it to player 1 to catch. They
   go back and forth until you call time.

4. **Lacrosse - Groundstroke Warm up** ....**15 minutes**
   Divide the players into two lines. One line hits forehand groundstrokes
   down the line. The other team uses the racket net to catch the other
   team's ball. If the team hitting groundstrokes gets a ball past the
   "lacrosse goalie," they score one point. If the goalie catches the ball, he
   scores one point for his team. After the completion of the game, switch
   to the backhand. Make sure everyone hits groundstrokes.

5. **Criss Cross Volleys**..**5 minutes**
   Separate the players into two lines at the service line. Player X1 crosses
   over and hits a backhand volley (right-handed player). X1 then goes to
   the end of the other line. X2 then crosses over and hits a forehand

volley (right-handed player) and then switches lines. Make sure the players split step, turn, step, and punch. This game can get exhausting for the children, so limit this drill to only five minutes.

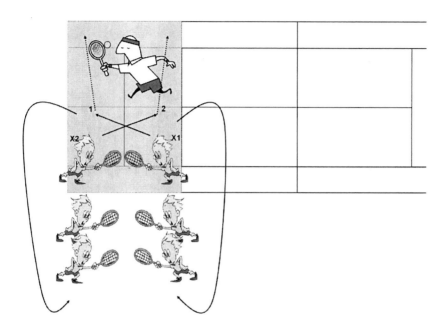

7-31 Criss Cross Volleys

6. **The Grand Prize Game**...5-10 minutes
Take a break from groundstrokes and volleys and work on the player's hand-eye coordination. Set out five empty hoppers two feet apart along the baseline. Have the player stand two feet away from the first hopper as he looks down the line of the hoppers. The player tosses the ball in the first hopper, if he makes it, he gets to try to toss it in the second hopper and so on. When the player misses he is out. Whoever gets a ball tossed into the farthest hopper, wins. Use low-compression balls as foam balls are too "bouncy." If the players are having a hard time making the ball in the hopper, use beanbags.

7. **Wrap up**...5 minutes
Recognize the bump up and down champions. Review how to keep score (love, 15, 30, 40, deuce, ad, game). There might be a test tomorrow for a prize!

Day 15 – Stroke of the Day: Introduction of the Full Motion Serve and Point Play Development

Equipment Needed: Funny hat, empty ball cans, flat targets, and low compression balls or foam balls

1. **Welcome/Take Roll**...3 minutes

2. **Warm up with the Line Game**..5 minutes
    Wear a funny hat today. For a prize, ask a volunteer to tell everyone how to keep score (love, 15, 30, 40, deuce, ad, game). Play the line game.

3. **Aerobic drill**..10 minutes
    Warm up the players' groundstrokes with the aerobic drill. Each player will hit a forehand down the line and then slide over and hit a backhand down the line. Go five minutes and then switch to backhand first and then sliding over to hit a forehand.

4. **Serve Warm up** ....5 minutes
    Review the mechanics of the serve. Have the players mirror you.

5. **Introduction of the Full Service Motion**......................5-10 minutes
    Spread the players out so they can mirror you as you demonstrate the full service motion.

    The following are the steps of a full service motion:

    1. Have player stand at a 45-degree angle to the net. Use teach feet to help his positioning.
    2. With his racket tip pointing to the target box, have the racket fall down to his side towards his right side (for a right-handed player). At the same time, the non-dominant hand comes down towards his left thigh.
    3. The racket now starts its way up along the right side bringing the racket head above the right shoulder. As the racket goes up, the non-dominant hand begins upward to toss the ball up. The right and left hand should be going up at the same time.
    4. The right arm now needs to be in a position similar to a quarterback throwing a football. The left arm is stretched as if trying to touch the sky.
    5. The player now reaches up to full extension to make contact.
    6. After contact, the racket falls to the left side of the body.

6. Bowling..10 minutes

Set out ten or more empty ball cans in one of the service boxes. Set them in a triangle similar to bowling pins. A player comes up and hits a full motion serve. (If the player struggles with the full motion, let him start the racket on his shoulder). The player gets a point for every "pin" he hits. If the player gets a strike, he automatically wins a prize. The player who hits the most "pins" after ten frames, wins!

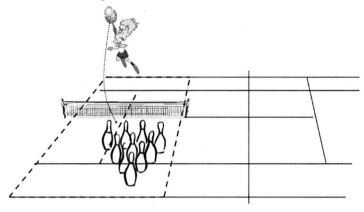

7-32 Bowling

7. Take Me Out to the Ball Game! ....15 minutes

Form two teams. Have one team "bat" and the other team in the field. Set out flat targets as bases. The batter has to hit the ball inside the court lines including the alleys. Balls hit outside of the court or in the net would

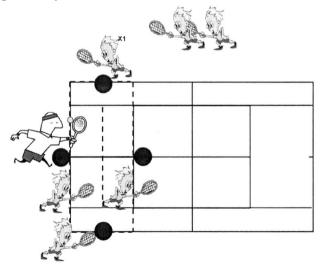

7-33 Take Me Out to the Ball Game

count as a foul ball. A player can "bunt" by moving up to the net and hitting a volley. When a player catches a ball, it is an "out." If players are having a hard time catching the ball in the air, allow the children to catch the ball after one bounce or let them use their hats or the racket net. You are the all-time pitcher. Make sure everyone gets a chance to bat.

8. **Team Around the World**...10 minutes

End the day with a fun game of Team Around the World. Divide the players into two equal teams. Have the players stand on the baseline of a 36' court. Separate the teams on each side of the court. Instructor feeds a ball to X1, who hits the ball and runs to the end of the line. X2 returns X1's ball and then goes to the end of the line. X3 returns X2's shot and goes to the end of the line. This goes on until someone misses a shot. When a player misses the shot, he sits down and is out of the game. The game will end when there are no players left on one of the teams.

7-34 Team Around the World

9. **Wrap up with Simon Says**...3 minutes

Play a game of Simon Says to end the day on a fun note! Thank everyone and let them know how to sign up for the next lesson series. Here are additional ideas to end the session; hire a snow cone truck to come out and give the players free snow cones or have a pizza party.

Lesson Plans for Ages 8-10

Day 1 – Stroke of the Day:
Introduction of Forehand Groundstroke

Equipment Needed: Funny hat, beanbag, low–compression balls, pee wee trainer, and field goal

1. Welcome/Take Roll..5 minutes

2. Follow the Instructor with the funny hat.....................3 minutes
   Wear your funny hat and wear it throughout the day. The kids will laugh at you and begin to loosen up.
   Jog around the court, jogging forward along the sidelines and shuffle your feet along the baselines. Teach the lines on the court as the players follow you. Have them copy your steps and repeat what you say about the lines.

3. Safety Position/Toss the Beanbag Over the River.......5 minutes
   Safety position – players hug their rackets pressing them against their chests. Inform the players that whenever they stand in line they need to put their rackets in safety position.
   Divide half the players along the single sideline facing the alley. Line the other half on the doubles sideline facing the alley. Pair up the players. Tell the players the alley is the Nile River full of alligators. Have the pairs toss a beanbag across the alley (river). The players have to toss the beanbag with their rackets and the other players have to catch it with their rackets. Challenge them by having them take one to three steps back.

4. Bump Ups and Downs...10 minutes
   Spread the players out on one side of the tennis court. Demonstrate how to bump the ball up on the racket with the palm up. Use low-compression balls.
   Have the players bump up, bounce, and bump up again with palms up. After a few minutes, switch to palm down. Progress to having the players simply bump up without the bounce.
   Challenge them to bump up while jumping on one foot.
   Demonstrate how to bump down with a low-compression ball with the palm down.
   Have the players bump down with the palm down.

5. Grip..5 minutes
   There are three options that seem to work best for teaching the forehand grip to this age group:

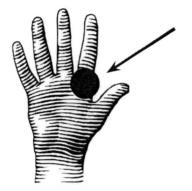

7-35
Base of Index Finger

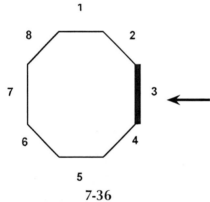

7-36
Eastern Grip Index Finger Placement

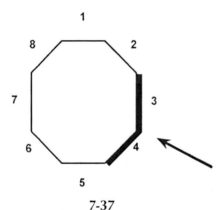

7-37
Hybrid Grip Index Finger Placement

Eastern Grip – base of your index finger should be on 3.

A. Belly Button Grip – The player puts the butt of the grip to her belly button with the racket head straight up and down where she can't see the strings. Then she puts her hand flat on the strings and slides the hand down to the grip.

B. Shake Hands Grip – First, shake hands with the player. Then take the player's racket, racket butt facing her and the head at the angle where you cannot see the strings, and have her shake hands with the racket.

Hybrid Grip - base of your index finger should be in between 3 and 4.

This grip is between the eastern (base of the index finger would be on 3) and the semi-western grip (base of the index finger would be on 4). It will shut the racket face just a bit to aid in topspin.

6. Stroke of the Day: Forehand Groundstroke.....5 minutes

Spread the players out on the baseline of a 60' court. Remember, players should have their rackets in safety position! Teach them the forehand groundstroke by using the Easy as 1-2-3 Short and Sweet or the Loopy Loop Method. Have the players begin with their sides turned in a stationery position rather than have them pivot and step. The players mirror you as you are swinging from position 1 to position 3.

7. Forehands with the Pee Wee Trainer .... **10 minutes**

Set up a pee wee trainer with dangling balls. Have the players turn their sides, rackets in position 1, and swing through to position 3. After contact, the players catch the balls and hit again. Challenge the players further by having them hit a ball swung by the pro. Make sure the players are praised for making contact and swinging through to position 3. You can never give enough "high-fives!"

8. Field Goal! Forehands with a Bounce .... **10 minutes**

Line the players up into one line at the baseline of a 60' court. Using low–compression balls, drop the ball in front of X1, allowing her to make contact in front. Note on the diagram where X2 is standing. Place a cone or a flat target to indicate where the line begins. This will help control the second player from getting hit with X1's backswing.

REMINDER:

If you do not have lines for the 60' court, the regular service line to "no-man's land" on a 78' court will be fine, however the use of tape for the lines will work.

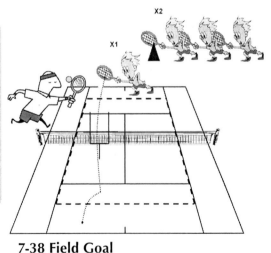

7-38 Field Goal

9. Wrap up – Give out Prizes .... **5 minutes**

Ask questions of the players for prizes, such as, *What was the stroke of the day? Can someone demonstrate a forehand grip?*

Day 2 – Stroke of the Day: Introduction of Backhand Groundstroke

Equipment Needed: Low–compression balls, field goal, cones, and pee wee trainer

1. **Welcome/Take Roll** .... **3 minutes**

2. **Outline the Court** .... **5 minutes**
   Run the lines on the court as shown in the diagram below. Teach the students the lines as they are running them.

7-39 Outlline the Court

3. **Bump Up and Down** .... **3 minutes**
   Spread the players out on one side of the court. Have them bump up for a few minutes and then bump down for a few minutes.

4. **Review Forehand – Field Goal!** .... **10 minutes**
   Using low–compression balls, bounce the ball in front of the player having them hit a forehand from position 1 to position 3 in between the poles for a field goal! Give each player three balls and then rotate. Have them keep their own scores. First player to ten wins!

7-40 Review Forehand

5. **Stroke of the Day: Backhand Groundstroke**............... 5 minutes

At this age, make it simple with the grip. Use the Eastern-Eastern grip for the backhand. Don't make it complicated by changing the right hand (for a right-handed player) for a two-handed backhand. As they progress and get into private lessons, you will know when it is time to change their grip. This is the time when the player needs to enjoy early success by making contact and not having to worry about grip changes.

Spread the players out on the baseline. Remember, players should have their rackets in the safety position! Teach them the backhand groundstroke by using the Easy as 1-2-3 method. Have the players mirror you as you swing from position 1 to position 3.

6. **Backhands with the Pee Wee Trainer**........................... 10 minutes

Set up a pee wee trainer with dangling balls. Have the players turn their sides, put their rackets in position 1 and swing through to position 3. After contact, the players catch the balls and hit again. Next, challenge the players by having them hit a ball swung by the instructor. Make sure the players are praised for making contact and swinging through to position 3. You can never give enough "high-fives!"

7-41 Pee Wee Trainer

7. **Balance the Racket!** ....5 minutes

This drill works on hand-eye coordination. Place half of the players on the single sideline and the other half on the doubles sideline. Have them face the players across from them at a slight angle. Have the players stand their rackets on the right side of their bodies with the racket heads touching the ground. The players across from them do the same thing, making sure the rackets are lined up directly across from their partners' rackets. When you say "Go!" the players let go of their rackets and run across the alley to catch their partners' rackets before they hit the ground. If both partners catch their rackets before they hit the ground, that pair receives one point. First pair to get to five wins!

Increase the difficulty by having one or both players take a step back.

> **SAFETY NOTE:**
> Make sure the players are not lined up directly across from each other. You don't want the players to run into each other. They should be at an angle.

8. **Backhands with a Bounce**.. 10 minutes

The players will hit from the baseline of a 60′ court. Using low–compression balls, drop the ball in front of the student allowing the player to make contact in front.

Note on the diagram where X2 is standing. Place a cone or a flat target to indicate where the line begins. This will help control the second player from getting hit with X1's backswing.

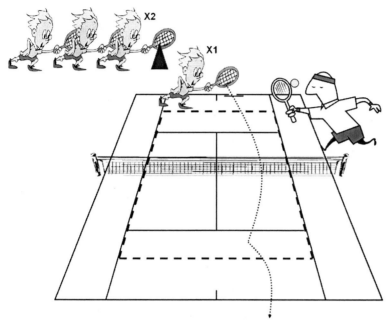

7-42 Backhands with a Bounce

> **NOTE:**
> Players will be hitting from the baseline of a 60' court. However, if a player is struggling from that distance, move her closer to the net.

9. **Line Game** .... 5 minutes

    Review the lines on the court. After reviewing the lines, line the players on the baseline. When you yell out a line, the players run to the line. If a player goes to the wrong line, she is out. As players get to know the lines better, increase the difficulty of the game by eliminating the last player to get to the line.

10. **Wrap up** .... 3 minutes

    Review the stroke of the day and ask questions for prizes, such as, *Can anyone name one major tennis tournament? Can anyone name one professional tennis player?*

Day 3 – Stroke of the Day:
Introduction of Volley

Equipment Needed: Low–compression balls, racket net, clown nose, foam balls, teach feet, and hula hoop

1. **Welcome/Take Roll**...**3 minutes**

2. **Warm-up with Caterpillar**...**5-10 minutes**

   Divide the group into two equal teams. Line one team behind the baseline, parallel to the singles sideline. Line the other team up on the other singles sideline on the same side of the court. Have all the players hold their rackets in front of them with their palms up. As shown below, X1 will roll her ball onto her neighbor's racket. After successfully passing the ball off, X1 will run behind her teammates to the beginning of the line. If one of the players drops the ball the team has to start over. First team to the net wins!

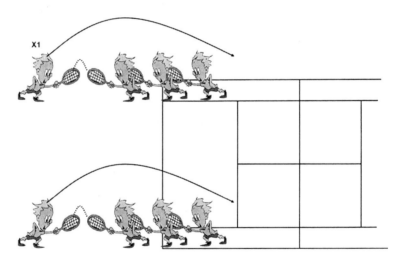

7-43 Caterpillar

3. **Review Forehand and Backhand Groundstrokes**

   Tennis Baseball...**10 minutes**

   Make sure players are lined up on the baseline of a 60′ court. However, if you have found your child or student is struggling from that distance, move her up to the service line. Continue to feed from same side as player, but move back, tossing the ball rather than simply dropping the ball in front of the child. Play with the instructor tossing low–compression balls to forehands for the first game. X1 hits a forehand. If the ball lands anywhere in the singles court, the player will remain "safe." If the player makes an error, she is "out" and has to run around to the other side of the net without her racket. The person who is "out" now tries to catch someone else's shot. If she does catch the ball, she returns to the "batting side" and replaces the player who hit the ball. Eventually there is only one player batting and the rest of the players trying to catch the shot. If the last player hits the ball in without getting the ball caught, she wins the game. If the last player misses the shot, he is now "out" and all the other players are now "safe." Change to backhands in the second game and alternate forehands and backhands in the third game.

7-44 Tennis Baseball

4. **Stroke of the Day – Volley** .... **5 minutes**

Spread the players along the net. Keep it simple and have the players keep the same Eastern grip that they use for the forehand groundstroke. This age group is old enough to learn to begin in "ready position." Start them in ready position, turn, step, and hit. If you find your group struggling with timing, have the players begin with their sides turned and then step and hit. Again, we want to make it as simple as possible for this age group.

On the backhand volley have the players use two hands for stability. Demonstrate how to hit a forehand and backhand volley as they mirror you. Remember, punch, don't swing!

5. **Volley – Racket Net**..**10 minutes**

Using the racket net, toss the ball softly to the player's forehand volley. Have the player start in ready position. Then she should turn, step, and catch the ball in the racket net. After two or three rotations, switch to the backhand volley.

6. **Hit My Nose! Volley with a Toss**....................................**10 minutes**

Wear a clown nose. Using foam balls, toss a ball to the player. The player hits a forehand volley trying to hit your clown nose. Set out teach feet to help guide her where to step. After two or three rotations, switch to backhand volleys.

7. **Volley Basketball**..**10 minutes**

Lay out a hula hoop at the service line on the opposite side of the court. Have the players keep track of how many "baskets" (hitting in the hula hoop) they make. First player to ten wins. Switch to the backhand volley. Remember, have the players turn, step, and hit.

8. **Wrap up with the Line Game**..**5 minutes**

Players line up at the fence. Yell out a line. The players then run to the line. If a player goes to the wrong line, she is out. As they get to know the lines better, increase the difficulty of the game by eliminating the last player to get to the line.

Day 4 – Stroke of the Day:
Introduction of Overheads and Serves

Equipment Needed:　　Funny hat, hopper, fishing pole, low–compression balls, teach feet

1. Welcome/Take Roll..3 minutes

2. **Ball Relay – Pro Wears a Funny Hat Today**.................**5 minutes**

Place three rackets along singles sideline and three more along opposite singles sideline on same side of the court. Form two teams. The first player from each team takes a ball out of the hopper (located at the center mark), runs, and puts the ball on the first racket. She then runs back to the hopper and gets another ball. She runs to the second racket and places the ball on the racket, and then she runs back to retrieve a third ball from the hopper. She runs to the third racket, places the ball on the racket and runs back to the line to tag the next player in line. The next player in line runs to the first racket and takes the ball off and puts it back into the hopper. He does this for the second and third racket. The next player in line then puts the balls back, one racket at a time. The drill goes on until the first team completes the drill and is declared the winner!

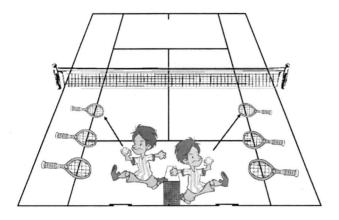

7-45 Ball Relay

3. **First Stroke of the Day: Overhead**.................................3 minutes

   Spread the players along the net. Make this stroke simple by having the players start with their sides turned and their rackets scratching their backs. Demonstrate the overhead while the players mirror you.

4. **Hitting Overheads with the Fishing Pole**.....................10 minutes

   Form a line and have the first player about three feet from the net hitting down on the ball. Make sure she starts with the racket back on her shoulder in the scratch back position. Each player hits three balls from the fishing pole. This drill works on overheads. It also works on their serving mechanics by teaching them to hit down and through the ball. Do five to seven rotations.

7-46 Overheads with the Fishing Pole

5. **Overheads with a Toss**...10 minutes
   Form a line and have the first player about three feet from the net. Toss the low-compression ball up as the player hits down on the ball. This drill is challenging the player by requiring her to time proper contact. Help her with the timing by saying, "toss and hit." Make it fun by dividing the group into two teams. When a player makes the shot, she scores one point for her team. First team to fifteen wins.

6. **Tennis Baseball**...5 minutes
   Take a break from overheads and play baseball.
   Make sure players are lined up on the baseline of a 60' court. Play with instructor tossing low–compression balls to forehands for the first game. Change to backhands in the second game and alternate forehands and backhands in the third game. (Continue to feed from same side as player.)

7. **Second Stroke of the Day: Serve** ....3 minutes
   Line the players along the service line or baseline of a 60' court. Teach them the difference between the deuce and ad box and teach them where they should stand when hitting a serve. Have the players mirror you as you explain how to hit a serve. At this point in their development, the players should start with rackets on their shoulders. It is not necessary to teach them the entire motion from starting position to the back scratch position. Remember, we want the players to have early success and starting with the rackets on their shoulders will speed up this success. To teach the grip, have the player put the racket completely on the ground and then have her pick it up. The palm should be up with the racket face open where the player can visualize putting a drink on the face like a waiter. You need to emphasize reaching to full extension and hitting up on the ball.

8. **Hitting Serves with the Fishing Pole** ....10 minutes
   The fishing pole is a great way to teach students to reach up on the serve and to make solid contact without the concern of throwing the ball toss in the proper spot. Have the players form a line at the baseline of a 60' court. However, it might be easier for your student or child to hit the serves from the service line. Let the players hit from the fishing pole three times and then rotate. Use teach feet to insure they are set up properly. Make it fun by doing the following variations which help them hit up on the ball:
   A. Have the players get on their knees and hit the fishing pole.
   B. Have the players get on their backs and hit the fishing pole.

9. **Serves with a Toss** ....10 minutes
   Forming a line at the service line or baseline of a 60' court, the first player will come up with her racket on her shoulder. Throw up the ball

toss with a low-compression ball. Have the player step on the teach feet to help show her where to stand. When the player is hitting the serve, her goals are to make solid contact and to have the ball clear the net. Make this drill fun by letting each student score a point if she hits the ball over the net and score two points if she hits the ball in the proper service box. First player to seven points wins a prize!

10. **Wrap up**..3 minutes
    Give out prizes to all the players for their great efforts throughout the session. Stickers, candy, and certificates are some ideas for prizes.

Day 5 – Stroke of the Day: Groundstroke Development

Equipment Needed: Funny hat, low–compression balls, field goal, and hula hoop

1. **Welcome/Take Roll**..3 minutes

2. **Follow the Instructor with the Funny Hat**..................3 minutes
    Put on a funny hat and wear it throughout the day.

    Jog around the court, jogging forward along the sidelines and shuffling your feet along the baselines. Have the players copy your steps. This is a great review of the lines on the court.

3. **Alley Rally!**..5-10 minutes
    This drill works on the players' motor skills and warms them up with their rackets in their hands. Have half the players line up on the singles sideline and the other half line up along the doubles sideline. The players from each line face each other. Place a ball just to the right of the player (if right-handed) about two feet in front of her. This will serve as the

7-47 Alley Rally

target for the player across from her. With rackets in their hands, palms up, they now bump the ball to each other trying to hit the ball in front of the player across them. If player hits the target (ball across from her), she gets one point.

4. **Groundstrokes – The 10-Point Club**............................. **10 minutes**

Players form a line at the baseline of a 60' court. With low–compression balls, feed four balls alternating to their forehands and backhands. Now feed on the other side of the net by tossing the ball. We want to challenge the players with the length of the feed. However, if the child is not ready, continue to feed on the same side. Make it fun for the players by adding a point to their total every time they make a shot. They are trying to get enough points to make it into the 5-point club and then the 10-point club and so on.

5. **Groundstrokes with Footwork** .... **3-5 minutes**

We are now challenging the players to move, set, and hit rather than hitting from a stationary position. Without their rackets, have the players form a line at the center of the baseline of a 60' court. Be on the other side of the net tossing a low-compression ball to the forehand side. The player moves over, lets the ball bounce, and then catches the ball. The player catches one ball and goes to the end of the line. Go through the line three to five times and then switch to the backhand. Go longer if players are having a hard time catching the ball.

7-48 Groundstrokes with Footwork

6. **Hit Recover – Field Goal!** .... **10 minutes**

    Continue to challenge the players' groundstrokes by having the them now move to the ball, set their feet, and hit the groundstroke. Make sure you emphasize that the child sets her feet. Have the player move from point A to point B and hit a forehand. Players hit three low–compression balls and go to the end of the line. A player scores one point if she hits it through the field goal. First player to ten wins! After approximately five minutes, rotate to backhands.

    At this point, I would hope the player naturally loads up in an open stance forehand. Some instructors might see a student in an open stance and make her turn her side because she is "too young." I believe if a player is athletic enough to hit in an open stance and is balanced, then let her stay in the open stance. However, in my experience, more players at this age feel more comfortable hitting in a square or closed stance. And if they're balanced, then that's fine.

7-49 Hit Recover

7. **Tennis Basketball** .... **10-15 minutes**

Set out a hula hoop three feet past the service box. Form a line at the baseline. Have the player move from point A to B and hit a forehand. If the player makes it in the service box, she scores one point. If she makes it in the hula hoop, then she scores two points.

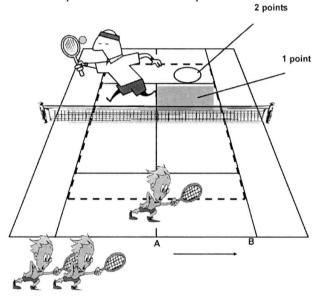

7-50 Tennis Basketball

8. **Wrap up**.. **3 minutes**

Ask the players questions for prizes, such as, *What is the most important stroke in the game of tennis? What is this line called?*

Day 6 – Stroke of the Day: Volley Development

Equipment Needed: Low–compression balls, teach feet, and a field goal

1. **Welcome/Take Roll**.. **3 minutes**

2. **Clean Your Plate**.. **5 minutes**

This popular drill is used for warming up players. Each player lays her racket down in a large circle with four balls on each racket. When the instructor says "Go!" each player takes one ball at a time off her racket and puts it on someone else's racket. They are trying to get their own racket (plate) empty. The first player to get an empty racket (plate) wins. This drill could go on for a while, so you might have to stop the drill once the players begin to tire.

3. **Review and warm-up volley** .... 10 minutes

   Review how to hit the volley, emphasizing contact in front of the body, and to punch (not swing).

   Divide the players into two lines. One line hits forehand volleys and the other line hits backhand volleys. Use low–compression balls and teach feet to insure they are stepping properly. After the player has hit three volleys, have her go to the end of the other line. Make sure the players start in ready position, and then they turn, step, and hit. You can make this drill fun by playing "10-point club." As they get better, challenge them by using a smaller target, such as the service box or a hula hoop. At the end of the lesson, give the players who made it into the 10-point club a sticker or a prize.

4. **Bus Driver** .... 10 minutes

   This game is only as fun as the instructor makes it. You'll toss the low–compression balls. Line the players along the net, spacing them out where they can hit a volley without hitting each other. The objective is to end up as the bus driver (X1) after a pre-determined time (i.e. five minutes). Toss a ball to any player. If the player misses, she moves to the end of the bus and all the players rotate up in line. You can make this game fun and exciting by looking one way and tossing the other. After the time is up, whoever is the bus driver is the winner!

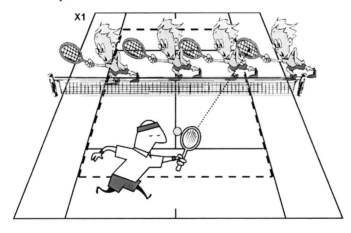

7-51 Bus Driver

5. **Side-to-Side Volleys** .... 10 minutes

   We now challenge the players by tracking the ball. The player will now move to the ball and hit the volley.

   Have the players form one line with the first player at the net. Feed four balls side-to-side alternating to the forehand volley and backhand volley.

After four balls, rotate. Make it fun by having the players try to join the "10-point club." Challenge the players by asking them to hit the ball past the service line.

6. **Hockey Tennis**...**10 minutes**

    Divide players into two teams. Set up a field goal approximately twelve feet behind the net and use low–compression balls. X2 is the goalie. Instructor feeds to X1. X1 is hitting a groundstroke trying to get the ball past the goalie through the field goal. If X2 hits a volley over the net and blocks the ball from getting through the goal, he scores two points for his team. If X2 blocks the ball from going through the net but misses the volley (i.e. hits it into the net), X1 scores one point for her team. If X1 hits it past the goalie and in the goal, she scores two points for her team. If X1 makes it in the court, but does not hit it in the goal, she scores one point for the team. After game is over, have the teams switch sides.

7-52 Hockey Tennis

7. **Line Game** ....**5-10 minutes**

    Review the lines on the court and play the Line Game.

8. **Wrap up – Simon Says** ....**5 minutes**

    Play Simon Says as a review. Remember, the instructor is the one who makes this game fun by being energetic and entertaining! Some examples Simon might say: *touch your feet, grip the racket at the throat, lift the racket over your head* and *show me a forehand volley.*

Day 7 – Stroke of the Day: Overheads and Serve Development

Equipment Needed: Field goal, fishing pole, low–compression balls, teach feet, and cones

1. Welcome/Take Roll ....3 minutes

2. Outline the Court ....5 minutes

Run the lines on the court as seen in the diagram below. Review the lines as players are running them.

7-53 Outline the Court

3. Review Groundstrokes – Field Goal! .... 10 minutes

This drill continues to challenge the players to move, set, and hit the ball. This is a great warm up drill for the players and keeps them from having to wait in a long line.

This is a fast drill that uses two low–compression balls. X1 hits a backhand, slides over to hit a forehand, and then goes to the end of the line. Reverse to the other side where the player hits a forehand first and then slides over to hit a backhand before going to the end of the line.

7-54 Review Groundstrokes – Field Goal

4. **Overhead Review** .... 3 minutes

   Review the mechanics of the overhead. At this point in their development, have the players start with the rackets on the backs of their shoulders. There is no need to have them swing the full motion at this stage.

5. **Overheads with the Fishing Pole** .... 5 minutes

   Form a line where the first player comes to the net and hits an overhead with the fishing pole. Have the player hit three overheads and rotate.

6. **Overheads with the Instructor's Toss** .... 5-10 minutes

   Form a line and have the first player about three feet from the net. You need to be approximately three feet away from the net on the other side of the court. Toss a low-compression ball up as the player hits down on the ball. This drill is challenging the players by having them time when to make contact. Help them with the timing by saying, "toss and hit." Make it fun by dividing the group into two teams. When a player makes the shot, she scores one point for the team. First team to fifteen wins.

   Challenge the players by moving back six feet, nine feet, and twelve feet when tossing the ball. You need to use good judgment to determine when and how far you should move back.

7. **Review the Serve** .... 3 minutes

Review the mechanics of the serve. At this point, do not teach them the full motion of the serve. They are still trying to develop timing while reaching up and making solid contact. The racket should start back on the shoulder.

> **NOTE:**
> If the players are struggling hitting serves from the baseline of the 60' court, move them up to the service line.

8. **Serve with a Pro's Toss** .... 5-10 minutes

Form a line and have the first player at the baseline of a 60' court. Throw up the low-compression ball for the ball toss. Have the player step on the teach feet. If you find the players having a hard time hitting the toss, pull out the fishing pole for a few rotations.

9. **Introduction of the Ball Toss – Basketball Lay-Up** ..... 5-10 minutes

Demonstrate the proper mechanics of the ball toss, including locating where the ball toss should land if you were to let it bounce. Have the players mirror you.

Take a cone and flip it upside down where the opening is facing the sky. Hold it in front of the player in the location where the ball toss should be when making contact. The player is tossing the ball up in a motion similar to a basketball lay up. They are trying to make it in the "basket." If they get the ball in the cone, they get a point. First player to five wins a prize!

10. **Hitting the Ball Toss** .... 5-10 minutes

The players are hitting from the baseline of a 60' court. Have two players come up to the baseline. Each player hits two serves using their own ball toss. At this point, players are still hitting serves with their rackets back on their shoulders. Make sure you teach them which box they should hit into.

11. **Wrap up** .... 3 minutes

Review what the players learned that day and ask a few questions for prizes, such as, *What are the names of the service boxes?*

Day 8 – Stroke of the Day: Footwork Development

Equipment Needed: Funny hat, hula hoop, field goal, and low–compression balls

1.   Welcome/Take Roll..3 minutes

2.   Hula Hoop Throw ....5 minutes
Instructor wears a funny hat today.

This is a great warm up, as well as a great motor skill drill. The instructor stands on the baseline with the hula hoop. The instructor rolls the hula hoop towards the net (the net will act as a back drop for the hula hoop to stop). Have a player on each side of the hula hoop. When the instructor roles the hula hoop, the two players play catch throwing the ball through the hoop as it is rolling to the net. To make it fun, pair up the players and see which pair can catch the most balls before the hula hoop touches the net and falls.

3.   Groundstroke Warm up – Field Goal!............................5-10 minutes
Players are without their rackets. To begin, toss a ball away from the player. Without her racket, she moves to catch the ball. If she catches the ball, she gets one point. The player then throws the ball through the field goal. If she makes it, she gets another point. Go a couple of times through and then switch to the backhand side.

Now with her racket, have the player move, set, and hit a forehand. Player scores one point if she hits it through the field goal. First player to ten wins! Player hits three low–compression balls and goes to the end of the line. After approximately five minutes, rotate to backhands.

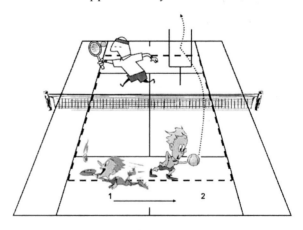

7-55 Groundstroke Warm up

4. **Focus of the Day: Footwork - Aerobic Drill**................. 10 minutes

Continue to challenge the players to move, set, and hit the ball. This is a great warm-up drill for the players and is beneficial to a large group by keeping the players from having to wait in a long line.

This fast drill uses low–compression balls. X1 hits a backhand, then slides over to hit a forehand and then goes to the end of the line. Reverse to the other side where the players hit a forehand first and then slide over to hit a backhand before going to the end of the line.

7-56 Aerobic Drill

5. **Warm up Overheads**..5 minutes

Do a quick warm up on overheads to lead into the next drill. Have the players line up at the net. The instructor is three to six feet away from the net on the opposite side tossing a ball to the player as she hits an overhead. Remember, the player should start with the racket on her shoulder.

6. **Groundstroke, Volley, and Overhead Drill** .... 10 minutes

This drill continues to work on footwork. Have the player move from A to B and hit a forehand groundstroke using low–compression balls. The player then moves from B to C and hits a forehand volley and then an overhead. This is a great time to teach the players the "split step." Go five minutes on the forehand side and then switch to the backhand side. Make it fun by playing to the 10-point club. Make sure you give the players a prize if they make it into the club!

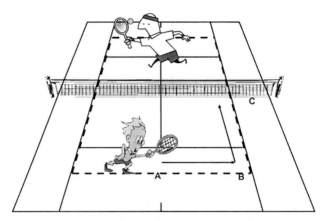

7-57 Groundstroke, Volley, and Overhead Drill

7. **Tennis Baseball**.. 10 minutes

   Play tennis baseball, tossing the ball out and away from the player, forcing her to move to her right, set her feet, pivot, and hit through the ball all the way to position 3. Feed to the backhand for the second game. For the third game, alternate feeds to the forehand and backhand.

8. **Side to Side – Hit My Funny Hat**..................................... 5-10 minutes

   Alternately feed each player four low–compression balls to the forehand and then to the backhand. The players are trying to hit your funny hat. If they hit it, they get a prize! After four balls, players rotate.

9. **Wrap up**.. 5-10 minutes

   Hand out prizes to all the players for their efforts throughout the session. If you use a skills chart, this is a great time to have the students put the stickers on the board. Make it visible so the parents can see. It will get the players excited to have their parents watch them put stickers on the skills chart.

Day 9 – Stroke of the Day:
Groundstroke Development and Point Play Development

Equipment Needed: Funny hat, low–compression balls, and hula hoop

1. **Welcome/Take Roll**.. 3 minutes

2. **Triangle Corner Relay** .... 5-10 minutes

   You will need four hoppers for this drill. Form two lines at the baseline. X1 takes two balls out of hopper-A. She then runs to hopper-B and places one of her two balls in there. She then runs to hopper-C where she places her last ball. She then runs back and tags the next player in line. First team to complete relay wins!

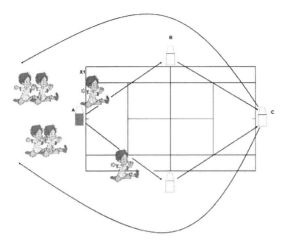

7-58 Triangle Corner Relay

3. **Side-to-Side Groundstrokes Warm up – Hit My Hat! ...5 minutes**

Have the players line up at the baseline of a 60' court. The first player comes in and hits four low–compression balls, alternating forehands and backhands. They are trying to hit your funny hat.

4. **Side-to-Side Groundstroke .... 5-10 minutes**

Player hits four low–compression balls, alternating forehands and backhands, and then rotates. The players should set their feet and hit. Keep the movement to the ball at a minimum. Again, have them try to hit your funny hat.

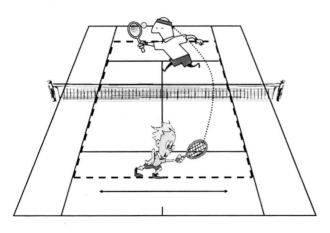

7-59 Side-to-Side

5. **Aerobic Drill with Fishing Nets**...................................... **10 minutes**

Continue to challenge the players by having them move and hit. Set out two 5' fishing nets. Weave them in the net so they will stand up. Set the fishing net where the students will have a target when hitting down the line. If player makes it into the fishing net, she scores one point. Using low–compression balls, the player hits a backhand down the line and then moves over to hit a forehand down the line. Go five minutes and then switch where the players hit a forehand down the line first and then slide over to hit a backhand down the line.

7-60 Aerobic Dril

6. **Hit Recover Cross Court - Tennis Basketball**.............. **10 minutes**

Instructor feeds away from the player forcing her to move, but with enough time to set her feet. Player hits a forehand with a low-compres-

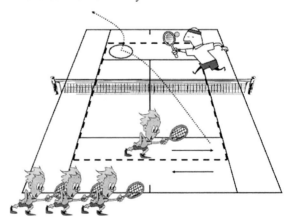

7-61 Hit Recover Cross Court

sion ball cross-court and then recovers back to the center. She is trying to hit it in the hula hoop. If the player hits it in the hula hoop, she scores two points. If she gets it cross-court, but not in the hula hoop, she scores one point. First player to ten wins! Switch to backhands after five minutes.

7.   RallyBall – Doubles .... 15-20 minutes
This is a great way to introduce point play at this stage of development. Divide into two teams and separate teams on each side of the court. Have two players from each team stand on the baseline of a 60' court. Feed the ball to X1. X1 hits the ball and plays out a doubles point. If X1 misses the feed, she gets a "second serve" (second feed). After the point or "second serve," players rotate. Teams are rewarded a point each time they make the ball in the court. The game emphasizes success on making a shot rather than winning a point. Have a parent or fellow instructor keep score. After everyone from a team receives a feed, feed to the other team and continue to rotate until ten minutes are up. Each set is timed ten minutes. Play two out of three sets.

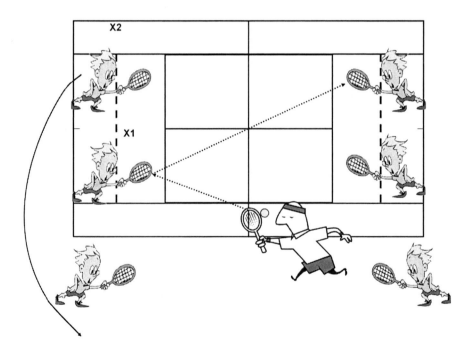

7-62 RallyBall – Doubles

8.   Wrap up with the Line Game .... 3-5 minutes

Day 10 – Stroke of the Day: Volley and Groundstroke Development

Equipment Needed: Low–compression balls and hula hoop

1. Welcome/Take Roll..3 minutes

2. Hula Hoop Role Warm up...5 minutes

   Form a line at the baseline. Then roll the hula hoop towards the net. The player runs beside the hula hoop sticking her foot inside and outside the hula hoop as it is rolling to the net. The player is trying to see how many times she can stick her foot in the hula hoop before it falls down at the net. After the hula hoop falls, the player brings it back to you. Whoever gets their foot in the hula hoop the most times wins!

3. Volley and Groundstroke Warm up – H-O-R-S-E......10 minutes

   The game H-O-R-S-E is played just like playing H-O-R-S-E in basketball. If the player misses the shot, she gets an "H", and so on until the word horse is spelled. Once horse is spelled, that player is out. Last player standing is the winner. Play H-O-R-S-E to the following drills:

   A. Forehand groundstroke cross-court
   B. Backhand groundstroke cross-court
   C. Forehand/backhand alternating cross-court
   D. Forehand volley cross-court
   E. Backhand volley cross-court

4. Criss Cross Volleys...10 minutes

   Separate the players into two lines at the baseline of a 60′ court. Player X1 crosses over and hits a backhand volley (right-handed player). X1 then goes to the end of the other line. X2 then crosses over and hits a forehand volley (right-handed player) and then switches lines. Make sure the players split step, turn, step, and punch.

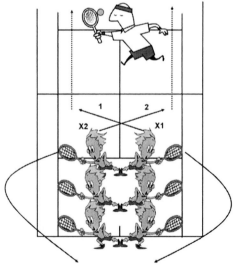

7-63 Criss Cross Volleys

5. **Groundstroke-Volley Combination**.............................. **10-15 minutes**

    Continue to challenge the players' groundstrokes and volleys with footwork. Have the players line up at the baseline. X1 comes in and hits a forehand groundstroke down the line. She then moves in, split steps, and hits a forehand volley. Make sure the player's body is under control when hitting the ground-stroke and then the volley. Don't get too quick with the feeds and make sure the players are set. If the player makes both shots down the line, she scores one point. First player to five wins! After five to seven minutes, change drill to the backhand side.

    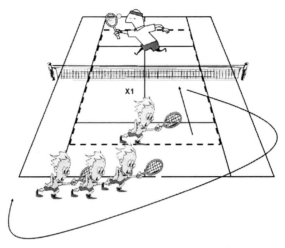

    7-64 Groundstroke-Volley Combination

6. **King of the Court - Play Points**...................................... **10-15 minutes**

    Players are now introduced to singles play. Divide the players into two groups. Instructor feeds with low–compression balls. Send half of the players to the "A" side and the other half to the "B" side. The only way to score a point is on the "A" side. If the player on the "B" side wins, the reward is to go on the "A" side where she can try to score points. If the player loses on the "A" side, she goes to the "B" side. First player to eleven wins!

    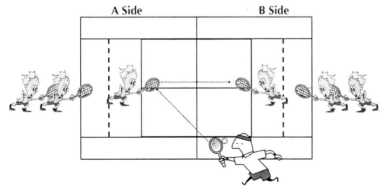

    7-65 King of the Court

7. **Wrap up**..5 minutes

Ask questions for prizes. Concentrate the questions to the highlights of the day such as single-point-play questions.

Day 11 – Stroke of the Day: Serve and Point Play Development, Keeping Score

Equipment Needed: Low–compression balls, teach feet, fishing pole, and circle target

1. **Welcome/Take Roll**..3 minutes

2. **Red Light, Green Light**..5-10 minutes

Have the players line up at the fence while you go to the net. When you yell "Green Light!" the players walk as fast as they can until you yell "Red Light!" First player to the net wins. Vary this drill by having the players do the following:

   A. Balance the ball
   B. Bump the ball down
   C. Bump the ball up

3. **Groundstroke warm up – Aerobic Drill**.......................10 minutes

Players continue to hit from the baseline of a 60' court. Using low–compression balls, X1 hits a backhand and then slides over to hit a forehand. Reverse to the other side where the players hit a forehand first and then slide over to hit a backhand after five minutes.

7-66 Aerobic Drill

4. **Serve warm-up** ....5 minutes

Warm up the player's serve by you tossing the ball toss. Have the player step on the teach feet at the baseline area. If you find any players having a hard time hitting the toss, pull out the fishing pole for a few rotations.

5. **Ball Toss Review – 5 Point Club** ....3-5 minutes

Have the players line up along the baseline of the 60' court. Have the players set up with their feet in position to hit a serve. Place a circle target at one o'clock. Have the players practice their ball toss without their rackets. If the ball comes down and hits the target, that player receives one point. Challenge the players to try to join the 5-point club by hitting the circle target.

6. **Hitting the Ball Toss/Introduction**
of Keeping Score ....15 minutes

Divide into two lines. Two players come up to the baseline. Players now toss their own ball and hit the serve into the proper box. Give each player two serves and then they rotate to the other line. Continue for five minutes.

Teach the players how to keep score. Begin with love, 15, 30, 40, deuce, ad-in, ad-out, game. The goal is for them to understand basic scoring by the end of the day. Don't overwhelm the players by getting into two out of three sets, tie-breakers, and match tie-breakers. At this age, it will be an accomplishment for them to learn the score in a game. As they progress and continue in your program, begin to introduce sets and tie-breakers. Continue for five minutes.

Form two teams. The first player from one team comes up and serves into the deuce box. The player from the other team comes in to serve to the ad box. If the player makes the serve (if the player misses, she gets a second serve), her team wins a point. The score is 15-love (if the player double faults, the score is love-15). If the next player makes it, the score would be 30-love. Continue until the game is complete. Play three or four times. Continue for five minutes.

7. **King of the Court with a Serve** ....15 minutes

Using a 60' court, divide players into two groups. The King of the Court side ("A") returns serves. This is the only side on which you can score points. The "B" side comes in and serves to start the point. The player gets a first and second serve. If the players are struggling, throw the ball toss for them. If they don't get the first or second serve in, begin the point for them by hitting a serve. If the player wins on the "B" side, she replaces the player she beat.

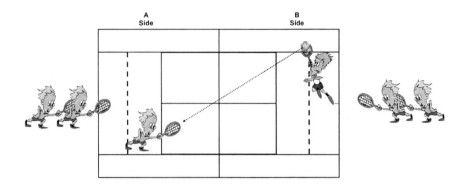

7-67 King of the Court

8. **Wrap up**..3 minutes
    Ask questions for prizes. This is a great time to test what they learned about keeping score.

Day 12 – Stroke of the Day: Full Motion Serve and Point Play Development

Equipment Needed: Funny hat, teach feet, and low–compression balls

1. **Welcome/Take Roll**...3 minutes

2. **Line Game**...5 minutes
    Instructor wears a funny hat today.

    Review the lines a final time while warming up the players. If a player gets confused and begins to run to the wrong line, she is out. Also, call out lines on the other side of the court. Add in the deuce and ad boxes.

3. **Side-to-Side Warm up – Try to Hit My Funny Hat**.....5 minutes
    Players will hit from the baseline of a 60′ court. First player comes up and hits four balls alternating forehands and backhands. Players are trying to hit the funny hat you're wearing. After four balls, the player rotates to the end of the line.

4. **Introduction of the Full Service Motion**......................5-10 minutes
    Spread the players out so they can mirror you as you teach them the full service motion.

    The following are the steps of a full service motion:

    1. Have player stand at a 45-degree angle to the net. Use teach feet to help her positioning.

2. With the racket tip pointing to the target box, have the racket fall down towards her right side (right-handed player). At the same time, the non-dominant hand comes down towards her left thigh.

3. The racket now starts its way up along the right side bringing the racket head above the right shoulder. As the racket goes up, the non-dominant hand begins to toss the ball upward. The right and left hand should be going up at the same time.

4. The right arm now needs to be in a position similar to a quarterback throwing a football. The left arm is stretched as if trying to touch the sky.

5. The player now needs to reach up to full extension to make contact.

5. **Serves** .... **10 minutes**

Players are working on the full service motion. Form two lines. Have two players come up to the baseline of a 60' court. Have one hitting to the deuce box and the other serving to the ad box. Each player gets two serves and then switches lines. Use teach feet and low–compression balls.

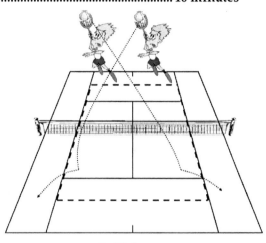

7-68 Serve

6. **RallyBall with a Serve** .... **10-15 minutes**

Divide into two teams and separate teams on each side of the court. Have X1 stand on the baseline of a 60' court. If player misses first serve, instructor feeds to X1 for "second serve." Play out the doubles point. After the point, have the players on both teams rotate. X1 moves to X2 spot, X2 goes to the end of the line, and X3 takes X1 spot. Same rotation for the other team. Teams are rewarded a point each time they make the ball in the court. The game emphasizes success on making a shot rather than winning a point. Have a parent or fellow instructor keep score. After everyone from a team hits a serve or receives a feed, switch to the other team and continue to rotate until ten minutes are up. Each set is timed ten minutes. Play two out of three sets.

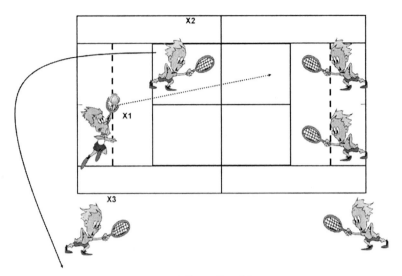

7-69 RallyBall with a Serve

7. **Team Around the World**.. 10 minutes

Divide the players into two equal teams. Have the players stand on the baseline of a 60' court. Separate the teams on each side of the court. Instructor feeds a ball to X1, she hits the ball and runs to the end of her line. X2 returns X1's ball and then goes to the end of his line. X3 returns X2's shot and goes to the end of her line. This continues on until someone misses a shot. When a player misses the shot, she sits down and is out of the game. The game will end when there are no players left on one of the teams.

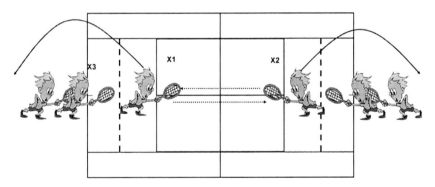

7-70 Team Around the World

8. **Wrap up**.. 3-5 minutes

Give prizes to everyone who participated in the program. Ask questions for additional prizes.

Day 13 – Stroke of the Day: Groundstroke Development

Equipment Needed: Low–compression balls, ball hopper, and ball machine

1. **Welcome/Take Roll**.. **3 minutes**

2. **Triangle Ball Pickup Relay**... **5 minutes**

   Divide players into two teams. Place six rackets on half of the court as shown in the diagram. First player from each team gets one ball out of the hopper and runs to the first racket. She places the ball on the racket and then runs back to retrieve a second ball. She runs to the second racket and places the ball there. She runs back to the hopper and does the same thing with a third ball. The second player runs to the first racket and takes the ball off and runs back and places the ball in the hopper. He does this for the second and third racket. The third player then places the balls back on the rackets, one ball at a time. First team to finish wins!

7-71 Triangle

3. **Groundstroke Warm-up**... **10 minutes**

   Use low–compression balls. The first player in line hits a backhand cross-court from the baseline of a 60' court. She then runs at an angle towards the service line and hits a forehand down the line. The player then goes to the end of the line. If the player successfully hits both shots in, she scores one point. See who can join the 10-point club. After five minutes, reverse to forehand cross-court and backhand down the line.

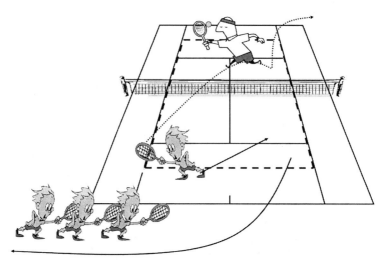

7-72 Groundstroke

4. **Jail** .... **10 minutes**

Use low–compression balls. Form one line with the first player hitting to the baseline. X1 hits a forehand anywhere in the singles court. If the X1 makes the shot, she goes to the end of the line. If the player misses, she has to go to jail. Jail is located on the other side of the net. A player can get out of jail by rallying a ball back successfully into the singles court. Two players in jail can attempt to hit the ball back at the same time. After one ball is hit, the players rotate in line. After five minutes, reverse to backhands.

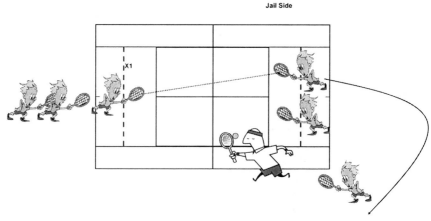

7-73 Jail

5. **Ball Machine Drill** .... 10 minutes
    The children will enjoy getting to hit balls fed by the ball machine. Make sure you set the speed on low so it will imitate your feeds. Have the players hit three balls and then go to the end of the line. A variation of this drill is to form a line on the other side of the net, hitting the ball back to the player who is hitting from the ball machine. This variation depends on how well your players are progressing.

6. **Racketless Tennis** .... 10 minutes
    Take a break from groundstrokes by playing a fun game of Racketless Tennis. Divide the players into two teams, A and B, where there are three players on each side of the court with no rackets. One player is at the net and two players are on the baseline. One of the players from Team A throws the ball trying to get it to bounce twice. If the ball bounces twice without Team B catching it, Team A wins a point. If the ball bounces once and a player catches it, no point is awarded. If the player at the net catches the ball without the ball hitting the ground, she wins a point for her team.

7. **Geography Tennis** .... 10 minutes
    Divide the players into two lines at the baseline. One line hits forehand groundstrokes and the other line hits backhands. Each section on the other side of the net is labeled a different state. For instance, one alley is Missouri, the other alley is Oklahoma, the deuce box is Kansas, the ad box is Indiana, and "no-man's land" is Texas. Players are trying to hit all five states. Each player gets two balls and then runs to the end of the other line. First player to hit a ball in every state wins a prize.

8. **Wrap up**... 3 minutes
    Review groundstrokes and inform everyone that tomorrow will be Team Spirit Day. Everyone wears the colors of her favorite college or professional team.

Day 14 – Stroke of the Day:
Team Day! Volley, Groundstrokes, and Point Play

Equipment Needed: Low–compression balls, cones, and flat targets

> **Special Note:**
> The children were told on the previous day of instruction to wear their favorite team colors. Today's theme is team tennis games and drills.

1. Welcome/Take Roll..3 minutes

2. Team Caterpillar..5 minutes
   Divide the group into pairs. Each pair is competing against the other pairs. The pairs need to be lined up side-by-side along the baseline. A player rolls a ball on her partner's racket and then goes in front of him to retrieve her ball. The players continue to roll the ball on their partners' rackets until they reach the net. If they drop the ball they have to return to the baseline and start over. First pair to the net wins!

3. Groundstroke/Volley Warm-up Minefield ....10 minutes
   Set out ten to twenty colorful cones on one half of the court (the more cones the better). Form one line. A player comes up and hits a forehand groundstroke cross-court trying to "explode" one of the mines (cones). She then moves in at an angle to hit a backhand volley down the line, again trying to "explode" a mine. After five minutes, move the cones over on the other half and have the players hit backhand groundstrokes and then forehand volleys. Give a prize to the player who explodes the most mines! Promote the winning player to Sergeant for the day!

4. Take Me Out to the Ball Game! ....15 minutes
   Form two teams. Have one team bat and the other team in the field. Set out flat targets as bases. The batter has to hit the ball inside the court including the alleys. A ball hit outside of the court and a ball hit in the net count as strikes. A player can "bunt" by hitting a volley. A player in the field catching a ball in the air creates an "out." The player can also be "out" if the outfield throws the ball to the first, second, or third baseman. You are the all-time pitcher. Make sure everyone gets a chance to bat.

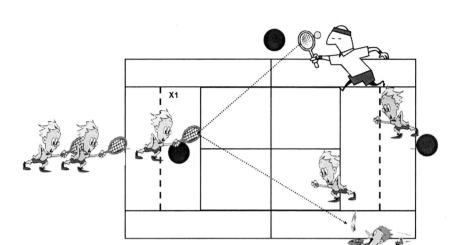

7-74 Take Me Out to the Ball Game

5. **Bus Driver** .... 10 minutes
Line the players along the net, spacing them out where they can hit a volley without hitting another player. The object is to end up as the bus driver after a pre-determined amount of time. Toss a low-compression ball to any player. If the player misses, she moves to the end of the bus and all players move up in line. Make the game fun and exciting. Looking one way and tossing the other way will keep the players on their toes. After the time is up, whoever is the bus driver is the winner! Challenge the players after a few games by having them hit the volleys past the service line. If they hit them inside the service line, they have to go to the end of the bus.

6. **Team Single Points** .... 15 minutes
This drill continues to work on point play ability. Divide the players into two teams. Two players come up and play out a singles point. When one player loses, she goes to the end of her team's line. The player who wins gets to stay in for another point and then regardless of win or lose, he goes to the end of his team's line. The players keep track of their points as a team. Play several games. Each player from the winning team gets a prize!

7. **Wrap up** .... 3 minutes
Recognize everyone who wore their favorite team's colors and give them a prize.

Day 15 – Stroke of the Day: Serves, Groundstrokes, and Point Play

Equipment Needed: Funny hat and low–compression balls

1. **Welcome/Take Roll**...3 minutes

2. **Warm up with the Line Game**...5 minutes
   Instructor wears a funny hat today.

3. **Aerobic Drill**...5 minutes
   This drill is a quick warm up using low–compression balls. Have the players line up hitting a forehand down the line and then sliding over to hit a backhand down the line. Go two to three minutes and then switch to a backhand down the line and sliding over to hit a forehand down the line.

4. **Serve Warm Up** ....5 minutes
   Review the full motion serve.
   Divide players into two lines hitting the serves from the same baseline of the 60' court. One line serves to the deuce box and the other line serves to the ad box. After two serves, players switch lines. Have them hit the serves using the full service motion. If players are struggling with timing, let them start with rackets on their shoulders.

5. **The Serve Game**..5 minutes
   Divide players into two teams. A player from each team comes up to the baseline of a 60' court to hit the serve. One team hits to the deuce box and the other team the ad box. Each player hits one serve and goes to the end of her line. A player scores one point for her team if she hits the serve in. The first team to ten wins. Have teams switch sides after one game.

6. **Team Around the World with One Racket**...................10 minutes
   Divide the players up into two teams with each team only having one racket. The first player hits the ball fed by the instructor to the other team. She then hands off the racket to the next player in line and then goes to the end of the line. If the player misses the shot, she is out. The other team does the same as they rally the ball back. Eventually, there will only be one team standing, and that team is the winner!

7. **Beat the Pro!**..10 minutes
   The children will love this game especially if they win a point off of the instructor. Form a line on one side of the net. One player comes up and plays one point versus the instructor. Each player only plays one point. If the player wins, she gets a prize!

8. **Work up with a Serve** .... 15 minutes

Spread the players out on multiple courts with two players on each court. For example, you will need three courts for six players. Players will play out points. Players who lost the previous point serve the next point. If they miss the first serve, they can drop and hit for the second serve. The players keep track of their points. After five minutes, rotate with the winners moving up a court and with the players who lost moving down a court.

Players who did not win move down

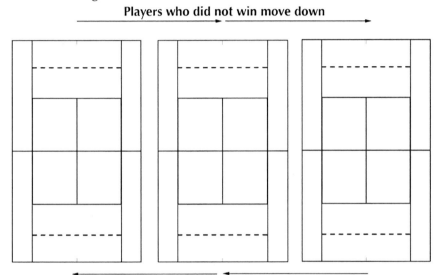

Winners move up

7-75 Work up with a Serve

9. **Wrap up with Questions** .... 3 minutes

Wrap up the session with questions serving as a review of everything the players have learned in this fifteen-day session. Such questions include, *Who can show me how to hit an Easy as 1-2-3 forehand?* or *Who can show me how to hit a full motion serve?* This is a great way to review everything the players learned through the program. Thank everyone and let them know when the next lesson series will begin, and how to sign up. End the session by giving your students a pizza party or by hiring a snow cone truck to come out and give the players snow cones.

8
Don't Let the Egg Drop!
Progressive Plans Games and Drills

Motor Skills, Footwork and More

Train

Focus: Footwork and learning the lines of the court

Equipment: Funny hat	Players: 1+

Description: Wear your funny hat. Kids will laugh at the hat and begin to loosen up. Have the kids form a line behind you. Have them follow you around all the lines on the court. While outlining all the lines, tell the players what the lines are. This is a good way to teach the lines of the court. Variations to the game are having the children jog, skip, march, or act like animals: crawling like a bear, flapping their arms like a bird, or hopping like a bunny.

Racket Control

Focus: Motor skills

Equipment: Foam balls, beach balls or low-compression balls and rackets	Players: 2+

Description: Have the players take a foam ball, beach ball or low-compression ball and balance it on their racket. Divide the players into two or three lines, depending on how many players you have in the group and have them relay. Players will walk fast or jog to a cone and back and tag the next player in line. The players balance the balls with their palms up for the first game and palms down for the second game. The first team to finish wins!

Hopper Relay

Focus: Motor skills

Equipment: Two hoppers, balls, and racket	**Players**: 4+

Description: Divide players into two teams. Set out two empty hoppers at the net and one hopper full of balls at the center mark. Each player will take a ball from the hopper, balance the ball on their racket with their palm up and place the ball into the empty hopper at the net. They then run back to their line and tag the next player. First team to get a predetermined amount of balls in their basket wins. After the relay is completed, play it again, but with the palm facing down. +

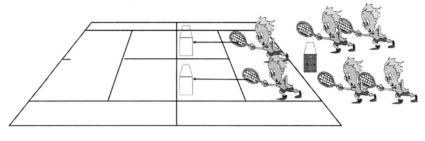

8-1 Hopper Relay

Line Game

Focus: Learning the lines on the court

Equipment: n/a	**Players**: 1+

Description: Teach the lines on the court. Players line up at the fence. Yell out a line. The players then run to the line. If a player goes to the wrong line, he is out. As players get to know the lines better, increase the difficulty of the game by eliminating the last player to get to the line. Variations to this game are having the players skip, hop, or balance balls to the lines.

"The Line Game is a great game that is fun, yet also makes the kids run, providing some conditioning."
Kayli Edwards, collegiate player who teaches tennis during the summers

Sandwich Relays

Focus: Motor skills

Equipment: Rackets, cones and balls	**Players**: 4+

Description: Divide the players into two lines. Two players from the same team sandwich a ball in between their rackets and race to the cone and back. If the players drop the ball, they have to start over. First team to complete the relay wins! A variation of this drill is to have the players sandwich the ball in between the grips of the racket—tough!

Beanbag Toss

Focus: Motor skills

Equipment: Beanbags and rackets	**Players**: 2+

Description: Working on hand eye-coordination, have half of the group spread out on the singles sideline and the other half spread out on the doubles sideline. Each player needs to be directly across from another player. Each player tosses a beanbag with his racket to the other player directly across from him. The player across the alley catches the bean bag with his racket. Tell the players they are tossing the beanbag over a river.

8-2 Beanbag Toss

Alley Rally!

Focus: Motor skills

Equipment: Low-compression or foam balls and rackets	**Players:** 2+

Description: Have half the players lined up on the singles side-line and the other half lined up along the doubles sideline, with the players from each line facing each other. Place a ball just to the right (right-handed player) of each the player, about two feet in front of him. This will serve as the target for the player across from him. With rackets in their hands (palms up) they now bump the ball to each other trying to hit the ball in front of the player across them. Players must let the ball bounce to bump the ball back. If player hits the target (ball across from him), he gets one point. After a predetermined time, the player with the most points wins!

8-3 Alley Rally

Don't Let the Egg Drop!

Focus: Motor skills

Equipment: Balls and rackets	Players: 2+

Description: Divide into two groups. X1 and X2 run to the net. As they are running, they are rolling a tennis ball on each other's racket back and forth. This drill continues to work on their motor skills. They have to concentrate on not dropping the ball off the racket as they are rolling it to each other's racket while on the move.

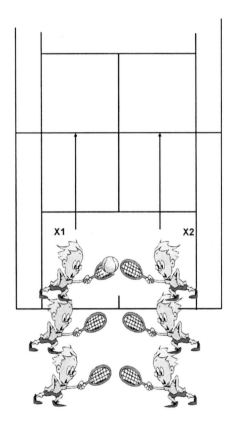

8-4 Don't Let the Egg Drop!

Simon Says

Focus: Motor skills

Equipment: n/a	Players: 1+

Description: This is a fun game that reviews what the players have learned throughout the classes. The following are a few Simon Says commands:

Touch your shoulders; Touch your hips; Forehand position 1; Backhand position 1; Backhand position 2.

Clean Your Plate

Focus: Motor skills

Equipment: Balls and rackets	Players: 4+

Description: This popular drill is used for warming up players. Each player lays his racket down in a large circle with four balls on each racket. Make sure the circle is large enough so players won't run into one another. When you yell, "Go!" each player takes one ball off his own racket and puts it on someone else's racket. Each is trying to get his own racket (plate) empty. The first player to get an empty racket (plate) wins. This drill could continue for a while, so you might have to stop the drill once the players begin to get tired.

Simon Says Line Test

Focus: Motor skills

Equipment: n/a	Players: 1+

Description: Play Simon Says by having the players run to the lines on the court, including the deuce and ad boxes. If the player runs to the line without Simon Says, he is out. Challenge the players by having Simon say a line or a service box on the other side of the court.

Caterpillar

Focus: Motor skills

Equipment: Balls and rackets	**Players**: 4+

Description: Divide the group into two equal teams. Line one team behind the baseline, parallel to the singles sideline. Do the same with the other team on the other singles sideline on the same side of the court. Have all the players hold their rackets in front of them with their palms up. X1 will roll his ball on his neighbor's racket. After successfully passing the ball off, X1 will run behind his teammates to the beginning of the line. If the players drop the ball, they have to start over. First team to the net wins!

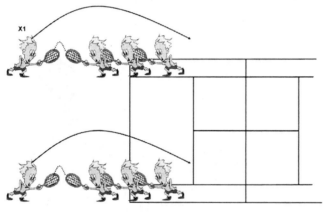

8-5 Catepillar

Red Light, Green Light

Focus: Footwork and motor skills

Equipment: If applicable, racket and balls	**Players**: 1+

Description: This is a great warm-up game. Have the players line up at the fence with the instructor at the net. When you yell "Green Light!" the players walk as fast as they can until you yell "Red Light!" First player to the net wins. Variations include running, skipping, hopping, balancing a ball, bumping the ball down, or bumping the ball up.

Balance the Racket!

Focus: Motor skills

Equipment: Rackets	**Players:** 2+

Description: Divide half the players on the single sideline and the other half on the doubles sideline. Have the players face each other at an angle in pairs. Each player stands the racket on the right side of his body with the racket head touching the ground. The player across does the same thing, but making sure the rackets are lined up directly across from the partners' racket. When the instructor says "Go!" the players let go of their rackets and run across the alley to catch their partners' rackets before they hit the ground. If both partners catch a racket before it hits the ground, that pairing receives one point. First pair to get to five points wins!

8-6 Balance the Racket

Racket Skills Relay

Focus: Motor skills

Equipment: Cones, rackets and balls	Players: 2+

Description: Divide players into two teams. Set out two cones, one for each line to run to. In game one, have the players bump the ball up to the cone and back. Game two, have the players bump down to the cone and back.

Follow the Pro with the Funny Hat

Focus: Footwork

Equipment: Funny hat	Players: 1+

Description: Jog around the court, jogging forward along the sidelines and shuffling your feet along the baselines. Teach the lines on the court as the players follow you. Have the players copy your footwork.

Bump Ups and Downs

Focus: Motor skills

Equipment: Low-compression balls and racket	Players: 1+

Description: Have the players bump up, bounce, and bump up again using low-compression balls with palms up. After a few minutes, have players switch to palms down. Proceed with the players bumping down with their palms down. Challenge them to bump up or bump down while jumping on one foot.

Ball Relay

Focus: Motor skills

Equipment: Ball hopper and rackets	Players: 2+

Description: Place three rackets along singles sideline and three more along opposite singles sideline on same side of the court. Form two teams. The first player takes a ball out of the hopper (located at the center mark) and runs to put the ball on the first racket and then runs back to the hopper and gets another ball. He runs to the second racket and places the ball on the racket and runs back to retrieve a third ball from the hopper. He runs to the third racket, places the ball on the racket and runs back to the line to tag the next player in line. The next player in line runs to the first racket and takes the ball off and puts it back into the hopper. She does this for the second and third racket. The next player in line will then put the balls back on the racket. This will go on until the first team to complete the drill is declared the winner!

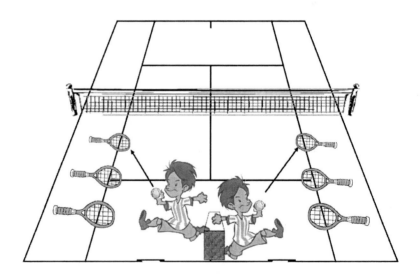

8-7 Ball Relay

The Grand Prize Game

Focus: Motor skills

Equipment: Hoppers, ball or bean bag	Players: 2+

Description: Set out five empty hoppers two feet apart along the baseline. Have the player stand two feet away from the first hopper as he looks down the line of the hoppers. The player tosses the ball in the first hopper, if he makes it, he gets to try to toss it in the second hopper and so on. When the player misses a hopper, he is out. Whoever gets a ball tossed to the furthest hopper wins. If players are having a hard time making the ball in the hopper, use beanbag

Outline the Court

Focus: Footwork

Equipment: n/a	Players: 1+

Description: Run the lines on the court as shown in the Diagram. Players will follow you or you can pick a leader. Teach the students the lines as they are running them.

8-8 Outline the Court

Hula Hoop Throw

Focus: Motor skills

Equipment: Hula hoop and a ball	**Players:** 2+

Description: Stand on the baseline with the hula hoop. Roll the hula hoop towards the net (the net will act as a back drop for the hula hoop to stop). Have a player on each side of the hula hoop. When you roll the hoop, the two players play catch (without a bounce) tossing the ball through the hoop as it is rolling to the net. To make it fun, pair up the players and see which pair can catch the most balls before the hula hoop touches the net and falls.

Keeping Score

Focus: Keeping score: Love, 15, 30, 40, deuce, ad, game

Equipment: Low-compression balls and rackets	**Players:** 2+

Description: Form two teams. The first player on Team A comes up and serves. If the player makes the serve, Team A wins the point, resulting in the score being 15-love regardless what the other team does. If the first player misses, he gets a second serve. If the player double faults, the score is love-15. The next player in line comes in to serve as the same rule applies. If the player makes it, the score would be 30-Love. Team B serves to the ad box. First team to "game" wins! After each game, switch sides.

Triangle Ball Pickup Relay

Focus: Motor skills

Equipment: Ball hoppers, low-compression balls and rackets	**Players:** 2+

Description: Divide players into two teams. Place six rackets on half of the court as shown in the diagram. First player from each team gets one ball out of the hopper and runs to the first racket. He places the ball on the racket and then runs back to retrieve a second ball. He runs to the second racket and places the ball there. Then he runs back to the hopper and does the same thing with a third ball. The second player runs to the first racket and takes the ball off and runs back and places the ball in the hopper. She does this for the second and third rackets. The third player places the balls back on the rackets one ball at a time. First team finished wins!

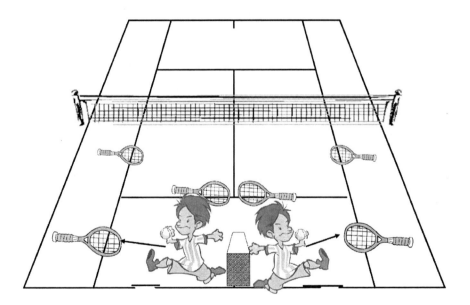

8-9 Triangle Ball Pickup Relay

Triangle Corner Relay

Focus: Motor skills

Equipment: Hoppers and balls	**Players:** 2+

Description: Form two lines at the baseline. X1 takes two balls out of hopper-A. He then runs to hopper-B, located at the net post and places one of his two balls in it. He then runs to hopper-C, located at the center of the other baseline and places his last ball in it. Finally, he runs back and tags the next player in line. Team B does the same thing but will run to hopper-D and hopper-C. First team to complete relay wins!

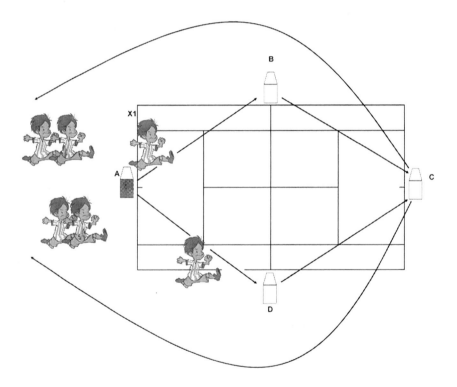

8-10 Triangle Corner Relay

Hula Hoop Warm Up

Focus: Motor skills

Equipment: Hula hoop	Players: 2+

Description: Form a line at the baseline. Roll the hula hoop towards the net. The player runs beside the hula hoop sticking his foot closest to the hula hoop inside and outside the hoop as it is rolling to the net. The player is trying to see how many times he can stick his foot in the hoop before it falls down at the net. After the hula hoop falls, the player brings it back to you. Whoever gets their foot in the hula hoop the most times wins!

Racketless Tennis

Focus: Motor skills

Equipment: Ball	Players: 6

Description: Divide the players into two teams where there are three players on each side of the court with no rackets. One player is at the net and two players are on the baseline. Any team member throws the ball anywhere on the court trying to get the ball to bounce twice. If the ball bounces twice without the other team catching it, that team wins a point. If the ball bounces once and a player catches it, no point is awarded. If the player at the net catches the ball without the ball hitting the ground, he wins a point for his team.

"A great game to improve many skills associated with tennis such as hand-eye coordination, footwork and throwing the ball which mimics the serving motion. A very fun game that will bring lots of laughs".
Marc Claude', USPTA Head Professional, on "Racketless Tennis"

The Million-Dollar Question!

Focus: Review of what the players learned that day

Equipment: n/a	Players: 2+

Description: Asking players simple questions for prizes is a great way to end a day of practice. It is also a good time to direct a question to the student who didn't win a prize through the practice. This way, he will go home with a prize, too. Target your questions around what you taught them that day such as, *Do you swing on your volleys?* Or, *What is the most important stroke in the game of tennis?*

Lesson Plan Games and Drills Groundstrokes

Groundstrokes with the Trainer

Focus: Forehand and backhand groundstrokes with a stationary ball

Equipment: Pee Wee trainer and racket	Players: 1+

Description: Set up a pee wee trainer with two dangling balls (see diagram). Have the players hit goundstrokes. Two players at the same time can hit off the trainer. After contact, each player catches the ball and hits again. Challenge the players by having them hit a ball swung by the instructor. Make sure the players are praised for making solid contact.

8-11 Pee Wee Trainer

Groundstrokes with a Bounce

Focus: Forehand and backhand groundstrokes with a bounce

Equipment: Foam balls or low-compression balls and racke	Players: 1+

Description: Line the players up forming one line at the service line or baseline of a QuickStart court. Using foam balls or low-compression balls, drop the ball in front of the student allowing him to make contact in front. Look for the player to make contact in front and not hit the ball late. It will help if your ball toss is in front of the student.

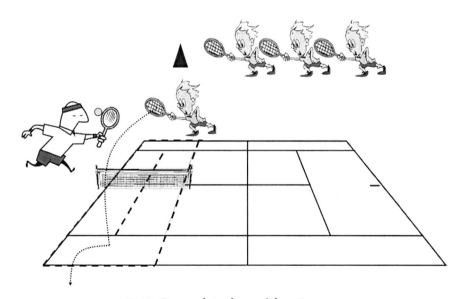

8-12 Groundstrokes with a Bounce

Field Goal!

Focus: Forehand and backhand groundstrokes

Equipment: Foam balls or low-compression balls, racket, and a field goal	Players: 1+

Description: Set up a field goal at the net. Using foam balls or low-compression balls, bounce the ball in front of the player having him hit a forehand or backhand groundstroke in between the poles for a field goal! As the players progress, move back, tossing the ball from a farther distance. Give each player three balls and rotate. Have them keep their own scores. Player scores one point per field goal. First player to ten wins!

8-13 Field Goal!

Tennis Baseball

Focus: Groundstrokes and motor skills

Equipment: Foam balls or low-compression balls and rackets	**Players:** 4+

Description: Players are lined up on baseline of a 36' or 60' court depending on the players' age and development. In the first game, play with the instructor tossing foam balls or low-compression balls to forehands. Change to backhands in the second game and forehands/backhands alternating in the third game. X1 hits a forehand. If the ball lands anywhere in the singles court, player X1 remains "safe." He goes to the end of the line. If he makes an error, he is "out" and has to run around to the other side of the net without his racket. The person who is "out" now tries to catch someone else's shot. If he does catch the ball, he returns to the "batting side" and replaces the player who hit the ball. Eventually you will have only one player batting and the rest of the players trying to catch the shot. If the last player hits the ball in without getting the ball caught, he wins the game. If the last player misses the shot, he is now "out" and all the other players are now "safe."

8-14 Tennis Baseball

"The most popular game at our club. A must for your program."
Tennis Instructor, on "Tennis Baseball"

Hit My Funny Hat

Focus: Groundstrokes

Equipment: Funny hat, low-compression balls, and racket	Players: 1+

Description: Stand on the other side of the net of the players and toss low-compression balls or foam balls as the players hit groundstrokes. Have them try to hit the funny hat on your head. Help them with the timing by saying, "bounce, hit" as they say it with you.

Hit Recover

Focus: Groundstrokes and footwork

Equipment: Low-compression balls and racket	Players: 1+

Description: Feed low-compression balls from the other side of the net. Have the player move from point A to point B, hit a groundstroke and then recover back to point A. You need to focus on the players setting their feet and then hitting the ball. Each player hits three low-compression balls and goes to the end of the line. Make it fun for the players by doing the 10-point club game.

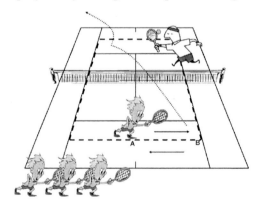

8-15 Hit Recover

Aerobic Drill

Focus: Groundstrokes and footwork

Equipment: Hula hoop (optional), 5′ fishing net (optional), low-compression balls, and racket	**Players:** 1+

Description: This is a fast-moving drill where the player hits two low-compression balls and goes to the end of the line. X1 hits a backhand and then slides over to hit a forehand. The player then goes to the end of the line. After a predetermined time, switch where the player hits a forehand down the line first and slides over to hit backhand down the line. The use of hula hoops as targets is an option, as well as placing two 5′ fishing nets weaved into the net as targets.

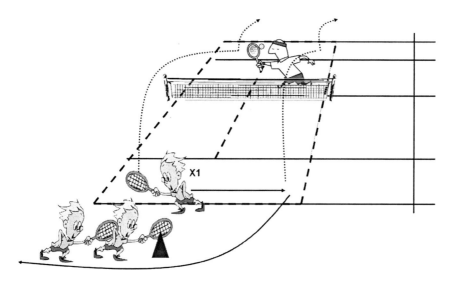

8-16 Aerobic Drill

Target Practice

Focus: Groundstrokes

Equipment: Hula hoop, field goal, low-compression balls, and racket	**Players:** 1+

Description: Set up the field goal and a hula hoop. Have the first player hit a forehand through the field goal and then slide over and hit a backhand in the hula hoop. If he makes it in the field goal or in the hula hoop, he scores two points for each shot made. He gets one point if he makes the shot in the court, but fails to make it through the field goal or in the hula hoop.

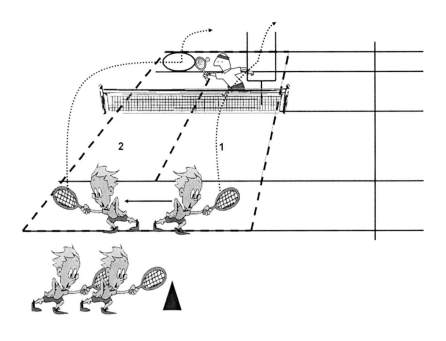

8-17 Target Practice

Team Around the World

Focus: Groundstrokes

| **Equipment:** Low-compression balls and rackets | **Players:** 4+ |

Description: This is a fun game! Divide the players into two equal teams. Separate the teams on each side of the court. Feed a ball to player X1. He hits the ball and runs to the end of his line. X2 returns X1's ball and then goes to the end of her line. X3 returns X2's shot and goes to the end of his line. This continues until someone misses a shot. When a player misses the shot, he sits down and is out of the game. The game will end when there are no players left on one of the teams.

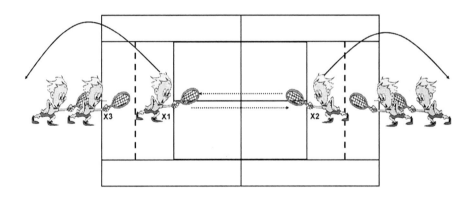

8-18 Team Around the World

"The number one game at our facility. We use it as a kick off to the day of instruction."

Tennis Instructor, on "Team Around the World"

Groundstroke Relay

Focus: Groundstrokes and footwork

Equipment: Low-compression balls and rackets	Players: 4+

Description: Divide the players into two teams and have them line up behind the baseline. The first players on each team run to the baseline of a 36′ or 60′ court. The instructor feeds the ball to the first player to reach the baseline and then to the other player. One team hits forehands and the other team hits backhands. The players hit the groundstroke and then tag the next player in line, regardless if they make the shot or not. After the game, have the team reverse sides. You can vary this game by not allowing the players to tag the next player in the line until they make the shot. Another variation: the first team to make 10 shots wins. A third variation is instead of the instructor feeding the balls, have the players run to the baseline and feed the balls themselves.

Team Groundstroke Points

Focus: Groundstrokes

Equipment: Low-compression balls and rackets	Players: 4+

Description: Divide into two teams. One team hits forehands groundstrokes and the other team hits backhands. Each team is hitting down the line in between the singles sideline and the center of the court. If the player makes the shot, he scores one point for the team. The first team to ten wins. A variation to this game is setting out two field goals or two hula hoops. If the player makes it through the field goal or in the hula hoop, he scores two points for his team.

Ball Machine Drill

Focus: Groundstrokes

Equipment: Ball machine, balls, and rackets	**Players:** 4+

Description: Set the ball machine on low speed simulating your feeds. Have each player hit three groundstrokes and then go to the end of the line. The Tennis Tutor Twist is a great machine that was specifically designed for this age group. A variation of this drill is to form a line on the other side of the net hitting the ball back from the player who is hitting from the ball machine. This variation depends on how well your players are progressing.

Tennis Basketball

Focus: Groundstrokes

Equipment: Hula hoop, low-compression balls, and racket	**Players:** 1+

Description: Set out a hula hoop three feet past the service box. Form a line at the baseline of a 36' or 60' court. Have the player move from point A to point B and hit a forehand. If the player makes it in the service box, the player scores one point. If the player makes it in the hula hoop, the player scores two points.

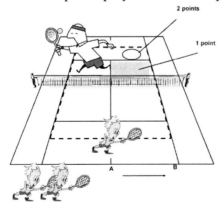

8-19 Tennis Basketball

Jail

Focus: Groundstrokes and motor skills

Equipment: Low-compression balls and rackets	**Players:** 4+

Description: Form one line. X1 hits a groundstroke anywhere in the singles court. If player X1 makes the shot, he goes to the end of the line. If the player misses, he has to go to jail. Jail is located on the other side of the net. A player can get out of jail by rallying a ball back successfully into the singles court. Two players in jail can attempt to hit the ball back at the same time. After one ball is hit, the players rotate in line.

Jail Side

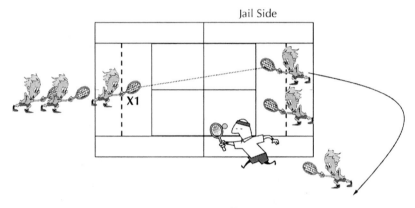

8-20 Jail

Team Around the World with One Racket

Focus: Groundstrokes and motor skills

Equipment: Low-compression balls and rackets	**Players:** 4+

Description: Divide the players up into two teams with each team only having one racket. The first player hits the ball fed by the instructor to the other team. He then hands off the racket to the next player in line and then goes to the end of the line. If the player misses the shot, he is out. The other team does the same as it rallies the ball back. Eventually, there will only be one team standing, and this team is the winner!

Geography Tennis

Focus: Groundstrokes

Equipment: Low-compression balls and rackets	**Players:** 2+

Description: Divide the players into two lines. One line hits forehand groundstrokes and the other line hits backhand groundstrokes. Each section on the other side of the net is labeled a different state. For instance, one alley is Missouri, the other alley is Oklahoma, the deuce box is Kansas, the ad box is Indiana and no-man's land is Texas. Players are trying to hit all five states. Each player gets fed two balls and then runs to the end of the other line. First player to hit a ball in every state wins a prize.

Lesson Plan Games and Drills
Volleys

Volley with the Trainer

Focus: Volleys

Equipment: Pee Wee trainer and racket	**Players:** 1+

Description: Using the pee wee trainer, swing the ball softly to the player's forehand or backhand volley. Make sure the player has his side turned with the racket in front of his body and punches. Have each player hit four volleys and then rotate.

Hit My Nose!

Focus: Volleys

Equipment: Clown nose, foam balls, and racket	**Players:** 1+

Description: Wear a clown nose. Using foam balls, toss a ball to the player and have him hit a forehand or backhand volley, trying to hit your clown nose. Set out teach feet to help him know where to step. Not only will the children get a kick out of you wearing a clown nose, but they will love trying to hit it with a foam ball.

Volley Basketball

Focus: Volleys

Equipment: Hula hoop, low-compression balls, and rackets	Players: 1+

Description: Set out a hula hoop. Feed three low-compression balls to each player and rotate. Players are trying to hit their volleys into the hula hoop. Have the players keep track of how many "baskets" they make. Each shot in the hula hoop scores one point. First player to ten wins! If players are struggling making it into the hula hoop, add one or two additional hula hoops.

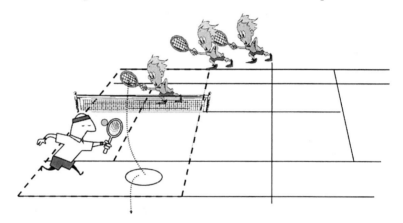

8-21 Volley Basketball

Volley Warm-up Drill

Focus: Volleys

Equipment: Low-compression balls and rackets	Players: 1+

Description: Divide the players into two lines, one line hitting forehand volleys and the other hitting backhand volleys. Use low-compression balls. After the players have hit three volleys, have them go to the end of the other line. As they get better, challenge the players by making the target smaller, like the service box or a hula hoop.

Bus Driver

Focus: Volleys

Equipment: Low-compression balls and rackets	**Players:** 4+

Description: This is a very popular game with students but it is only as fun as the instructor makes it. Toss low-compression balls. Line the players along the net, spacing them out where they can hit a volley without hitting each other. The objective is to end up as the bus driver (X1) after a pre-determined time (i.e. five minutes). Toss the ball to any player. If the player misses, he moves to the end of the bus and all the players rotate up in line. Make the game fun and exciting. Looking one way and tossing the other way keeps everyone on their toes. After the time is up, whoever is the bus driver is the winner!

8-22 Bus Driver

Field Goal! Side-to-Side Volleys

Focus: Volleys and footwork

Equipment: Low-compression balls and rackets	**Players:** 1+

Description: Set a field goal approximately six feet on the other side of the net. Have the players hit forehand and backhand volleys alternating feeds to each side. Players hit four low-compression balls trying to hit the ball through the field goal. Player then goes to the end of the line. Have them try to make the 10-point club or 20-point club, depending on how well they are progressing.

Bean Bag Volleys

Focus: Volleys and racket control

Equipment: Bean bag and racket	**Players:** 1+

Description: Divide the players into two lines. One line hits forehand volleys and the other line hits backhand volleys. Toss a bean bag to the player. Teach the players racket control and not to swing. The player catches the bag on her racket and then tosses it back to the instructor. A variation of this game is to have players tossing the bean bag to a teammate as they are trying to catch it on their racket.

Side-to-Side Volleys

Focus: Volleys and footwork

Equipment: Low-compression balls and rackets	**Players:** 1+

Description: Have the players form one line with the first player at the net. Feed four balls side to side alternating to the forehand volley and backhand volley. After four balls, rotate. Make it fun by having the players try to join the "10-point club." Challenge the players by having them hit past the service line.

Criss-Cross Volleys

Focus: Volleys and footwork

Equipment: Low-compression balls and rackets	Players: 4+

Description: Separate the players into two lines at the service line. Player X1 crosses over and hits a backhand volley (right-handed player). X1 then goes to the end of the other line. X2 then crosses over and hits a forehand volley (right-handed player) and then switches lines. This game can get exhausting for the children, so limit this drill to only five minutes or less.

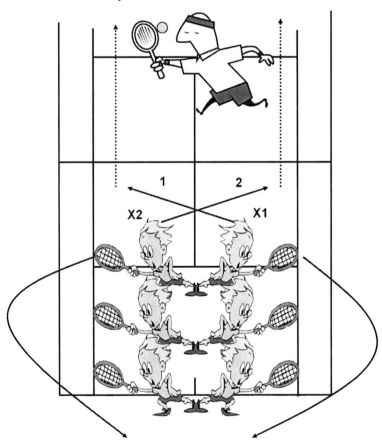

8-23 Criss-Cross Volleys

Lesson Plan Games and Drills
Serves and Overheads

Hitting Serves with the Fishing Pole

Focus: Serves

Equipment: Fishing pole and rackets	**Players:** 1+

Description: The fishing pole is a great tool to teach students to reach up on the serve and to make solid contact without the difficulty of throwing the ball toss in the proper spot. Have the players form a line and let the players hit from the fishing pole three times and then rotate. Use teach feet to insure their feet are positioned properly. Make it fun and help them hit up on the ball by doing the following variations:
* Have the players get on their knees and hit the fishing pole.
* Have the players get on their backs and hit the fishing pole.

Serves with an Instructor's Toss

Focus: Serves

Equipment: Foam balls or low-compression balls and rackets	**Players:** 1+

Description: Forming a line at the baseline of a 36′ or 60′ court, the first player will come up with his racket on his shoulder. Instructor will throw up the ball toss with a foam ball or low-compression ball. When the player is hitting the serve, the goals are to make solid contact by reaching up to full extension and clearing the net. Make this drill fun by keeping score. Students score one point if they hit the ball over the net and they score two points if they hit the ball in the proper service box. First player to seven points wins a prize

Overheads with the Fishing Pole

Focus: Overheads

Equipment: Fishing pole and rackets	**Players:** 1+

Description: The instructor holds the fishing pole in front of the student designating where the ball would be for an overhead. Form a line and have the first player about three feet from the net hitting down on the ball. Make sure player starts with the racket back on the shoulder in the scratch back position. This drill works on overheads. It also works on serving mechanics by teaching them to hit down and through the ball.

Overheads with Instructor's Toss

Focus: Overheads

Equipment: Low-compression balls and rackets	**Players:** 1+

Description: Form a line and have the first player about three feet from the net. The instructor tosses the low-compression ball up as the player hits down on the ball (the instructor needs to be approximately three feet away from the net on the other side of the court). This drill is challenging the player by requiring him to learn proper timing for contact. Help him by saying, "toss and hit" at the proper time. Make it fun by dividing the group into two teams. When a player makes the shot, he scores one point for his team. First team to fifteen wins. As players get better, challenge them by moving back six feet, nine feet, and twelve feet when tossing the ball.

Basketball Lay-Up

Focus: The service ball toss

Equipment: Cone and balls	**Players:** 1+

Description: Take a cone and flip it upside down where the opening is facing the sky. Hold it in front of the player in the location where the ball toss should be when making contact. The player is tossing the ball up in a motion similar to a basketball lay up. They are trying to make it in the "basket." If he gets the ball in the cone, he gets a point. First player to five wins!

Hitting the Ball Toss

Focus: Serve

Equipment: Low-compression balls and rackets	**Players:** 1+

Description: Form two lines and have two players come up to the baseline of a 36' or 60' court. Each player hits two serves using his own ball toss. After the two serves, players switch lines. Players are hitting the serves with their rackets back on their shoulders. Make sure you remind them which box they should hit into.

The Serve Game

Focus: Serves

Equipment: Low-compression balls and rackets	**Players:** 4+

Description: Divide players into two teams. A player from each team comes up to hit a serve. One team hits to the deuce box and the other team hits to the ad box. Each player hits one serve and goes to the end of his line. A player scores one point for his team if he hits the serve in. The first team to score ten points wins. Have teams switch sides after one game.

Bowling

Focus: Serving

Equipment: Empty ball cans, low-compression balls, and rackets	**Players:** 2+

Description: Set out ten or more empty ball cans in one of the service boxes. Set them in a triangle similar to bowling pins. A player will come up to the baseline of a 36′ or 60′ court and hit a serve. The player gets to add as many points to their total as the number of "pins" they hit. If the player serves a "strike," he automatically wins a prize. The player who hits the most "pins" after ten frames wins!

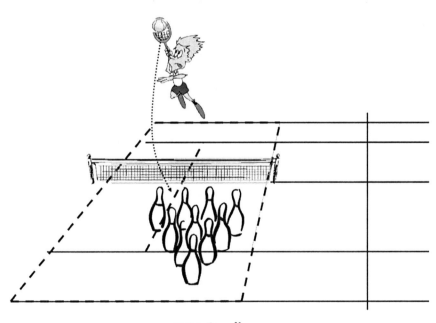

8-24 Bowling

Lesson Plan Games and Drills Multiple Strokes

Hockey Tennis

Focus: Groundstrokes and volleys

Equipment: Field goal, low-compression balls, and rackets	**Players:** 2+

Description: Divide players into two teams. Set up a field goal approximately twelve feet behind the net and use low-compression balls. If you do not have a field goal, two cones will also work. Player X2 is the goalie. Instructor feeds to player X1. X1 is hitting a groundstroke trying to get the ball past the goalie to the field goal. If X2 hits a volley over the net and blocks the ball from getting through the goal, she scores two points for her team. If X2 blocks the ball from going through the net but misses the volley (i.e. hits it into the net), the player scores one point for her team. If X1 hits it past the goalie and in the goal, he scores two points for his team. If X1 makes it in the court, but does not hit it in the goal, he scores one point for his team. After game is over, have the teams switch sides.

8-25 Hockey

The 10-Point Club

Focus: Groundstrokes, volleys, and serves

Equipment: Foam balls or low-compression balls and rackets	Players: 4+

Description: Form a line. Feed four balls alternating to player's forehand and backhand. Every time a player makes a shot, he adds a point to his total. Player's goal is to get enough points to join the 5-point club and then the 10-point club and so on. You can vary the game with the players hitting serves or volleys.

Groundstrokes and Volley Combination Drive

Focus: Groundstrokes, volleys, and footwork

Equipment: Teach feet or flat targets, low-compression balls, and rackets	Players: 1+

Description: Set up teach feet or flat targets to indicate where the players will run to hit their shots. The player will hit a groundstroke and then proceed in a straight line to the next spot to hit a volley. After the volley, the player goes to the end of the line. This is a simple warm-up drill and moves pretty fast, so players don't have to wait in line long. Make sure when they get to the target they set their feet.

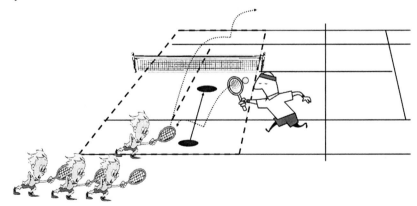

8-26 Groundstrokes and Volley Combination Drive

Groundstroke – Volley with Footwork

Focus: Groundstrokes, volleys, and footwork

Equipment: Low-compression balls and rackets	**Players:** 1+

Description: Have the player move from A to B and hit a forehand groundstroke, then move from B to C and hit a forehand volley. This is a great time to teach the players the "split step." Go five minutes on the forehand side and then switch to the backhand side. Make it fun by doing the 10-point club. Make sure you give the players a prize if they make it into the club!

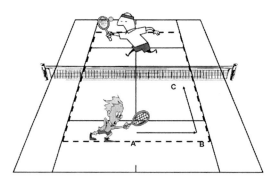

8-27 Groundstroke with Footwork

H-O-R-S-E

Focus: Groundstrokes, volleys or serves

Equipment: Low-compression balls and rackets	**Players:** 2+

Description: The game H-O-R-S-E is played just like playing H-O-R-S-E in basketball. If the player misses the shot, he gets an "H," and so on until H-O-R-S-E is spelled. Once H-O-R-S-E is spelled that player is out. Last player standing is the winner. Play H-O-R-S-E to the following drills:
* Forehand groundstroke crosscourt
* Backhand groundstroke crosscourt
* Forehand/backhand alternating crosscourt
* Forehand volley crosscourt
* Backhand volley crosscourt
* Serves

Take Me Out to the Ball Game!

Focus: Groundstrokes, volleys, footwork, and hand-eye coordination

Equipment: Flat targets, low-compression balls, and rackets	Players: 1+

Description: Form two teams. Have one team "bat" and the other team in the field. Set out flat targets as bases. The batter (X1) has to hit the ball inside the court including the alleys. A ball hit outside of the court and a ball hit in the net count as strikes. A player can choose to "bunt" by moving up and hitting a volley. A player in the field catching a ball in the air creates an "out." A player is also out if the first, second and third basemen tag the player out. If players are having a hard time catching the ball in the air, allow the children to catch the ball after one bounce. The instructor is the all-time pitcher. Make sure everyone gets a chance to bat.

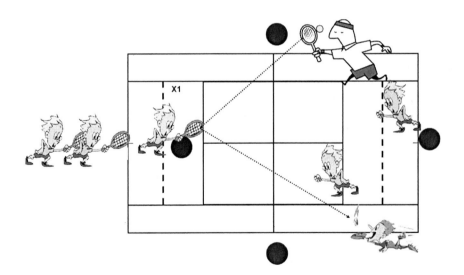

8-28 Take Me Out to the Ball Game!

Groundstrokes, Volleys, and Overhead Drills

Focus: Groundstrokes, volleys and overheads

Equipment: Low-compression balls and rackets	**Players:** 1+

Description: Have the player move from A to B and hit a forehand groundstroke. The player then moves from B to C and hits a forehand volley and then an overhead. Go five minutes on the forehand side and then switch to the backhand side. Make it fun by doing the 10-point club. Make sure you give the players a prize if they make it into the club!

8-29 Groundsroke, Volley and Overhead Drill

Minefield

Focus: Groundstrokes, volleys or serves

Equipment: Cones, low-compression balls and rackets	**Players:** 1+

Description: Set out ten to twenty colorful cones on one half of the court (the more cones the better). Form one line. A player comes up and hits a forehand groundstroke crosscourt trying to "explode" one of the mines (cones). He then moves in at an angle to hit a backhand volley down the line, again trying to "explode" a mine. After five minutes, move the cones over on the other half and have the players hit a backhand groundstroke and then a forehand volley. A variation to this game is to set all of the mines in the service box and have the players serve trying to explode the mines. Give a prize to the player who explodes the most mines! Promote the winning player to Sergeant for the day!

Lesson Plan Games and Drills
Point Play

RallyBall – Doubles

Focus: Groundstrokes and point play

Equipment: Low-compression balls and rackets	Players: 4+

Description: This is a great way to introduce point play for beginners. Divide into two teams and separate teams on each side of the court. Have two players from each team stand on the baseline of a 36′ or 60′ court. Feed the ball to player X1. X1 hits the ball and plays out a doubles point. If X1 misses the feed, he gets a "second serve" (second feed). After rally has completed, a new player comes in to take X1's spot and X1 moves to X2's spot and X2 goes to the end of the line (same rotation for other team). Teams are rewarded a point each time they make the ball in the court. The game emphasizes success in making a shot rather than winning a point. Have a parent or fellow instructor keep score. After everyone from a team receives a feed, feed to the other team and continue to rotate until ten minutes are up. Each set is a timed ten minutes of play. Play two out of three sets. Vary the game by having the players serve. If the player misses the serve, you can feed the ball to the player for the second serve.

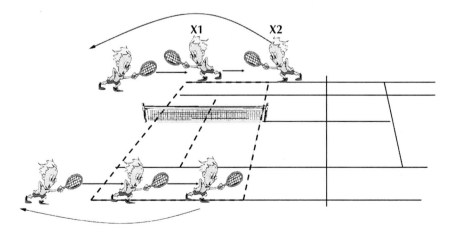

8-30 RallyBall

King of the Court

Focus: Point play

| **Equipment:** Low-compression balls and rackets | **Players:** 3+ |

Description: Divide the players into two groups, half on the A side of the court and the other half on the B side. Instructor feeds with low-compression balls. The players can only score a point on the A side. If the player on the B side wins, the reward is to move to the A side where he can try to score points. If the player loses on the A side, he goes to the B side. Have the players start out at the baseline of a 36' or 60' court. First player to eleven wins! Vary the game with the player serving or feeding the ball.

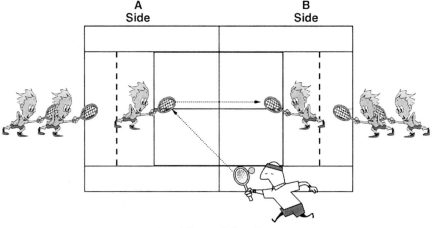

8-31 King of the Court

Beat the Pro!

Focus: Point play

| **Equipment:** Low-compression balls and racket | **Players:** 1+ |

Description: Form a line on one side of the net. One player comes up to the baseline of a 36' or 60' court and plays a point against the instructor. Each player only plays one point. Players will enjoy this game for the simple fact they are playing against their instructor. Make it fun, by making a "big deal" when a player beats you! If the player wins, he gets a prize.

Lacrosse

Focus: Groundstrokes and racket control

Equipment: Racket net and low-compression balls	**Players:** 2+

Description: Divide the players into two lines. One line hits forehand groundstrokes down the line. The other team uses the racket net to catch the other team's ball. If the team hitting groundstrokes gets a ball past the "lacrosse goalie," it scores one point. If the goalie catches the ball, he scores one point for his team. After the completion of a game, switch to backhand groundstrokes. Make sure everyone hits groundstrokes.

Team Single Points

Focus: Point playing

Equipment: Low-compression balls and rackets	**Players:** 4+

Description: Divide the players into two teams. Two players come up and play out a singles point. When one player loses, he goes to the end of his team's line. The player who wins gets to stay in for another point and then regardless of win or lose, he goes to the end of his team's line. The players keep track of their points as a team. Each player from the winning team gets a prize!

Work up with a Serve

Focus: Point playing

Equipment: Low-compression balls and rackets	**Players:** 4+

Description: Spread the players out on multiple courts with two players on each court. For example, you will need three courts for six players. Players will play out points. Players who lost the previous point serve for the next point. If they miss the first serve, they can drop and hit for the second serve. The players keep track of their points. After five minutes, rotate with the winners moving up a court and the losers moving down a court.

Team Single Points Variation

Focus: Point playing

Equipment: Low-compression balls or foam balls, and rackets	Players: 4+

Description: Divide into two teams. Use one 36′ court if you have 5 or less players and use two 36′ courts if you have 6-8 players. Players feed their own ball to begin the point. As seen on the diagram, the teams are divided by an 'A' team on one side and the 'B' team on the other side. Each court plays out 2 out of 3 points. The winning player, X1, runs to the hopper full of balls, grabs one ball, puts it into his team's hopper and then goes to the end of his team's line. The player who did not win, X3, goes to the end of his line. X1 is replaced by X2 and X3 is replaced by X4. The same format applies for players X5 and X6. Play two out of three 5-minute sets. After the five minutes are up, call time and count how many balls the teams have in their hoppers. Whichever has the most balls, wins that set. This game moves quickly and reduces standing in line for a long period of time.

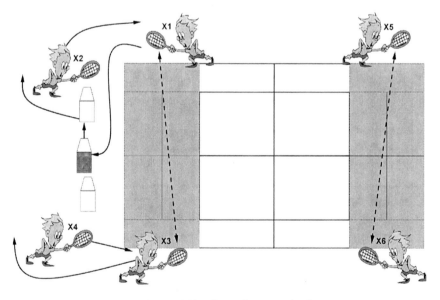

8-32 Team Single Points Variation

9
Wiggle Those Hips
More Innovative Games and Drills

Cloud Toss

Focus: Motor Skills

Equipment: Balls	**Players:** 4+

Description: Cloud Toss can be played with seven or fewer players. The instructor holds one less ball than players in the group. For example, if you have seven players, hold six balls. The players surround you as you throw all the balls straight up in the clouds. The players are trying to catch a ball to stay in the game. If a player doesn't catch or retrieve a ball, she is out. On the next throw, again hold one less ball in your hand than players left in the group. Eventually there will only be one player standing as the winner!

Musical Rackets

Focus: Motor Skills

Equipment: Rackets and balls	**Players:** 5+

Description: Set the player's rackets in a circle. Use one less than you have in the group; if you have six players, set out five rackets. The players form a circle outside of the rackets each holding a ball. When you yell, "Go!" players walk in a circle around the rackets. When you yell, "Stop!," players put a ball on the racket next to them. One player will be eliminated because she doesn't have a racket to put her ball on. Now take out one racket. Continue until there is only one player left standing! The game is best played if you have music, but if not, instructor can simply shout, "Stop!"

Hot Potato

Focus: Motor Skills

| **Equipment:** Balls | **Players:** 5+ |

Description: Have the players form a circle. Start out with two balls (hot potatoes). The players toss the balls to one another. When you call "Time!" the two players with a ball in their hands are out. When you get down to four players, use only one ball. The last player standing without a ball in their hand wins!

Darts

Focus: Groundstrokes

| **Equipment:** Hula hoop, cones, low-compression balls, and rackets | **Players:** 1+ |

Description: Set out a hula hoop representing the bull's-eye where the service line and center service line meet ("T"). Surround the hula hoop with cones, forming a circle. Leave about four feet between the cones and the hula hoop, forming a "dart board." Players are hitting groundstrokes. If the player hits inside the hula hoop, she gets 50 points. If she hits in between the hula hoop and the cones, she is awarded 25 points. After a pre-determined time, the player who has the most points wins!

Fishing Net Serves

Focus: Serves

| **Equipment:** Fishing net pole, low-compression balls, and rackets | **Players:** 1+ |

Description: You'll need a fishing net on a pole that is five feet long. Weave the handle in and out of the tennis net holes, keeping the fishing net raised two feet over the tennis net. The player serves with low-compression balls and tries to hit the ball in the fishing net. If the player gets the serve in the fishing net, she gets one point. The player with the most points win!

Bump and Catch

Focus: Hand-eye coordination; Groundstroke control

Equipment: Low-compression balls and rackets	**Players:** 2+

Description: After teaching groundstrokes, separate the players into pairs. Have half of the players line up along the doubles sideline with their rackets. Their partners, without rackets, line up four feet on the outside of the singles sideline. Each player without a racket gets a ball. The partner tosses a ball to their teammate. The teammate bumps the ball back as their partner tries to catch the ball. If they bump and catch successfully, they score one point. After a predetermined time, the pair with the most points wins. Have players switch after the completion of the first game. Note: Demonstrate to the children how to bump the ball with their racket head open and under control rather than hitting the ball hard.

Wiggle Those Hips Relay

Focus: Warm-up and conditioning

Equipment: Cones, balls, and rackets	**Players:** 4+

Description: Divide players into two teams. Players line up where the baseline and single sideline meet. Set out two cones, one on each singles sideline three feet from the net for the players to run towards. Players balance a ball on their rackets, running to the cone. When they get to the cone, they have to wiggle their hips and then run back to the line to tag the next player. This is a great game. It gives parents, children, and instructors a good laugh.

Bass Fishing

Focus: Volleys

Equipment: Racket net	**Players:** 1-5

Description: Form a line where the first player comes up catching her volley with the racket net. This teaches the children not to swing, but rather punch as they stick their racket up where the ball is to catch the "fish" (ball).

Tennis Hockey Variation

Focus: Hand-eye coordination and footwork

Equipment: Cones, balls, and rackets	**Players:** 6+

Description: Using only half the tennis court, set out two cones at the net about eight to ten feet apart. Do the same at the baseline. Divide the players into two teams. The children's rackets serve as their hockey sticks and the ball as their puck as they try to score goals. Players roll the ball on the ground with their rackets. The area past the doubles sidelines is out-of-bounds. If a player is able to get a ball through the cones, her team scores one point.

T-E-N-N-I-S

Focus: Spelling, groundstrokes, volleys, or serves

Equipment: Low-compression balls and rackets	**Players:** 2+

Description: You can do this drill with any type of stroke including groundstrokes, volleys, and serves. The game is played like "P-I-G" or "H-O-R-S-E" in basketball. Each time the player makes the shot, the players gets a letter. The younger players learn how to spell the word, "TENNIS." Play this game using different words such as serve, volley, forehand, and backhand.

Onesies, Twosies, Threesies

Focus: Hand-eye coordination

Equipment: Balls and rackets	Players: 2+

Description: Line the players up at the service line area or closer. Drop one ball in front of the player. If the player makes the shot, she is a onesie. Next time the player comes up, drop two balls in front of her at the same time. The player tries to hit both of the balls over the net. The balls are still alive as long as they don't roll. The player can continue to attempt to scoop the balls up and hit them over. If the player is successful hitting both balls over the net, they are a twosie. Continue on with threesies, foursies, etc.

Multiplication Tennis

Focus: Multiplication, groundstrokes, volleys, or serves

| **Equipment:** Low-compression balls and rackets | **Players:** 6+ |

Description: Parents will be impressed that you implement multiplication in this drill. You can do this drill with any type of strokes including groundstrokes, volleys, and serves. Use low-compression balls. Each time the player makes a shot, she gets one point which the player multiplies by two and receives two points. If the same player hits another shot in, she then multiplies two points times two which equals four points and so on, always multiplying by two. A variation of this drill is to do addition. If the player makes the shot in Round 1, she gets one point. If she makes the shot in Round 2, she adds one point (made in Round 1) to two points. If in Round 3 the player makes the shot, she adds three points to her current total (3 plus 2, 1, or 0). This is a drill good for 9 and 10-year-olds.

Roll

Focus: Team work, hand-eye coordination, and footwork

| **Equipment:** Rackets and balls | **Players:** 6+ |

Description: Separate the players into two teams, one team on each side of the court. Spread the players out on both sides of the court. The object of the game is to not let the ball roll. Put the ball into play by hitting a high lob to one side of the court. To avoid confusion, a player has to call for the ball. That player then hits the ball to the other side of the net. If the ball doesn't make it over the net and rolls, the other team wins one point. The players can avoid the ball rolling by scooping the ball up and hitting it back across the net or passing the ball to a teammate and letting her hit the ball over the net.

Tennis Soccer

Focus: Warm-up, motor skills, and footwork

Equipment: Cones and balls	Players: 6+

Description: Using only half the tennis court, set out two cones at the net about 8-10 feet apart. Do the same at the baseline. Divide the players into two teams. The players use the tennis ball as the soccer ball. Players roll the ball on the ground by kicking it. The area past the doubles sidelines is out-of-bounds. If a player is able to kick a ball through the cones, her team scores one point.

Flag Tennis

Focus: Motor skills

Equipment: Flag football flags or rags, rackets, and balls	Players: 6+

Description: Separate players into two teams. Use only half of the court, lining up one team along the net and the other team along the baseline. Each player needs to wear a flag. One team wears a solid color flag and the other team wears a white flag. For the flags you can use flag football flags or rags. While balancing a ball on their rackets, players are trying to get flags from the other team. If a player's flag is pulled, or if she drops the ball, she is out. Play until there are no players left on a team. If you don't have flags, have the players tag each other.

Piñata

Focus: Hand-eye coordination

Equipment: Piñatas and rackets	Players: 4+

Description: This is a fun game to play at the conclusion of a session. Purchase a piñata at your local party store. Let the players--one at a time--take shots at the piñata with their rackets. Once the piñata is broken, and the candy falls out, let the children run and collect all the candy. This is a great conclusion to a session while all the parents watch the excitement of the kids getting candy!

Candy Factory

Focus: Groundstrokes, volleys, or serves

Equipment: Candy wrappers, cones, low-compression balls, and rackets	Players: 2+

Description: Collect as many cones as you have in inventory and get old candy wrappers and tape them in the inside of the cones. Gather all the cones and put them in one area, such as the deuce box, so it will be easier for the children to hit. If a player hits a cone, the player runs over to see what type of candy bar she won by looking inside the cone. At the end of the day, the player takes the wrappers and redeems them for the candy bars they won. Players will be excited to hit a cone and find out what kind of candy they won. Instructor can do this game with groundstrokes, volleys, or serves.

Around the World

Focus: Groundstrokes and conditioning

Equipment: Low-compression balls and rackets	Players: 6+

Description: Divide the children into two lines, one line at each baseline. Feed a low-compression ball to one of the lines. Player A hits the shot and then runs to the other side of the court. The player receiving the ball hit by player A returns the shot and runs to the other side of the court. When a player misses the shot, she is out. When you get down to two players, they simply play out a point without running to the other side.

Feeding the Lion

Focus: Forehand groundstroke feeding

Equipment: Teaching basket, low-compression balls, and rackets	Players: 1+

Description: This drill works on the player's ability to feed the ball. Set out a teaching basket across the net in the service line area. Tell the players they are trying to feed the great big lion. Have all the players roar like a lion if one of the players makes the low-compression ball into the basket and successfully feeds the lion.

Serve Against the Fence Drill

Focus: Serves

Equipment: Balls and rackets	Players: 1+

Description: This drill works to improve the players' reach when making contact with the ball on their serves. Spread the players along the fence. The players, facing the fence, will start with their rackets on their shoulders and toss the ball up close to the fence. The player then reaches up to the ball and tries to catch the ball in between the racket and the fence.

Bounce and Balance

Focus: Hand-eye coordination

Equipment: Regulation tennis balls and rackets	Players: 1+

Description: Form two lines so two players can go at the same time. Toss the balls into the air. After a predetermined number of bounces the players are challenged to catch and balance the ball on their rackets. For example, if the instructor says, "Four," the player has to let the ball bounce four times before catching and balancing the ball.

Triathlon

Focus: Forehand and backhand groundstrokes, volleys, and serves

Equipment: Low-compression balls and rackets	Players: 4+

Description: You will need three instructors for this game. Each instructor will be feeding and monitoring a station. The first station is a forehand or backhand groundstroke. If the player hits the ball successfully back, she runs to the second station, which is the volley station. If the player makes both a forehand and backhand volley, she then runs to the third and final station, the serving station. When the player makes the serve, she then finishes the triathlon. If she misses in any station, she goes to the end of the line of that station and tries again. A player cannot move to the next station until she completes current the station successfully.

Alley Rally Variation

Focus: Racket control

Equipment: Hopper, low-compression balls, and rackets	Players: 1+

Description: Have the players line up on the doubles sideline. Set an empty hopper on the singles sideline. Toss a ball in front of the player. The player lets the ball bounce and then bumps the low-compression ball in the hopper. If successful, she gets a point. First player to score ten points wins.

The Grand Prize Game Variation

Focus: Racket control and feeding

Equipment: Hula hoops, low-compression balls, and rackets	Players: 2+

Description: Set out five hula hoops along the baseline, each hula hoop touching one another. The player stands two feet away from the first hula hoop and feeds a ball with her racket into the hula hoop. If she makes the first shot, she tries to make it in the second hula hoop and so on. If the player misses, she is out. The player who gets the ball to the furthest hula hoop is the winner! You can challenge the players by spreading the hula hoops out one foot apart.

Gotcha

Focus: Groundstrokes, volleys or serves

Equipment: Low-compression balls and rackets	Players: 4+

Description: Form one line. The first player hits a groundstroke. If the player makes the shot, the next player in line must make the shot or she is out. If the second player in line makes the shot, then it is carried over to the third player in line where he has to make the shot or he is out. As players get better, challenge them by hitting the groundstroke further away or having them move, set, and hit. A variation of this game is having the players hit volleys or serves.

Keeping Score

Focus: Learning to keep score, groundstrokes, volleys, or serves

Equipment: Low-compression balls and rackets	**Players:** 2+

Description: This game replaces any game that uses single digit points. Instead of playing to a certain predetermined number, have the players keep score, using love, 15, 30, 40, deuce, ad, and game. Line the players up in one line. The player hits one groundstroke and goes to the end of the line. If the player makes the shot, she gets 15 and if she makes the next shot, she gets 30 and so on until "game." A variation to this game is challenging the player by shortening the court or having them hit to a certain area. You can also play this with volleys and serves. This is a great warm-up game that will keep their interest since there is competition involved.

Bombs Away

Focus: Lobs and footwork

Equipment: Racket nets, low-compression balls, and rackets	**Players:** 4+

Description: Divide the players into two teams. One team, The Bombers, is hitting lobs off the instructor's feeds and the other team is standing on the other side of the court at the baseline. The team on the baseline is trying to catch the ball with their racket nets or their hands. The bombers score a point if the lob lands past the service line and inside the baseline. The team on the baseline scores a point if they catch the ball. The children will love this game!

Hopscotch Tennis

Focus: Footwork, groundstrokes, or volleys

Equipment: Chalk or tape to outline hopscotch diagram, low-compression balls and rackets	**Players:** 2+

Description: Outline a hopscotch diagram with chalk or tape on the court. Form one line. The first player comes up and hops through the hopscotch diagram and then runs to the baseline of a 36' or 60' court and hits a groundstroke. A variation to this drill is to have the player run to hit a volley.

Tag

Focus: Motor skills and footwork

Equipment: Balls and rackets	**Players:** 4+

Description: Spread the players out on half the court. Designate one player as "It." Everyone has to balance a ball on her racket. When you say "Go!" the player who is "It" tries to tag a player. If a player drops her ball, gets tagged, or runs outside the lines, she is also "It." Keep players moving and excited. End game after a predetermined amount of time.

Backboard Darts

Focus: Feeding and groundstrokes

Equipment: Tape, low-compression balls, and rackets	**Players:** 1+

Description: Using tape, outline a picture of a round target similar to a dartboard on the backboard. Have the players begin by standing seven feet away from the backboard. Have the players continue to move back as you feel they are ready. The first player comes up trying to feed the ball in the target. If the player hits the center of the target, she gets five points. If the player hits the target, but not the center, she gets one point. Player with the most points wins!

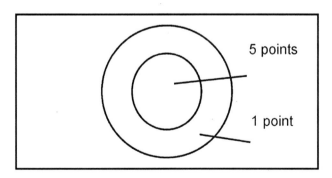

9-1 Backboard Darts

Select References

Daniel R Gould, Larry Lauer, Cristina Rolo, Caroline Jannes and Nori Pennisi, *Understanding the role parents play in tennis success: A national survey of junior tennis coaches*, BMJ Publishing Group Ltd & British Association of Sport and Exercise Medicine, 2006

Carol L. Otis, M.D., *USTA High Performance Coaching Newsletter*, Vol 6, No. 1, US Tennis Association, 2004

Tennis Catalog, Pages 25-27, HEAD/Penn Racquet Sports, 2006

Credits

Derek Boyer photo by permission of Derek Boyer
Matt Carter photo by permission of Matt Carter
Lexia Chen photo by permission of Lexia Chen
Anthony Gomez photo by permission of Anthony Gomez
Mark Lucas photo by permission of Mark Lucas
Emma Powell photo by permission of Emma Powell

Greg Mason attributions by permission of Greg Mason, Senior
Director of Sales, HEAD/Penn Racquet Sports Penn Tennis 2006
catalog pg 25-27

Sally Schwartz attributions by permission of Sally Schwartz, USPTA
and PTR professional with Canyon Creek Club in Richardson, Texas

Index

Index

Get More!

Sizzle Up Your Next Tennis Event:

Contact David and discover new ways he can support your tennis team, fund-raiser, club, and community.

Email or Call Today

David Minihan: David@westwoodtennis.com 405-366-8859

Consumer Copies:

Go to MansionGroveHouse.com for a current list of retailers and discount offers for copies of *Coaching Your Tennis Champion: The Progressive Plan for Success*. Also available through leading chain and independent bookstores, online retailers, tennis pro shops, sporting goods stores, and catalogs.

Visit Today
MansionGroveHouse.com

Reseller Copies:

Distributor, Retailer & Tennis Group Inquiries to:
Email: sales@mansiongrovehouse.com
Phone: 408.404.7277
Fax: 408.404.7277
Website: mansiongrovehouse.com

Be Empowered

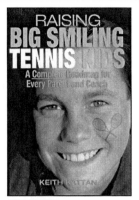

ISBN 1932421114
2006 Second Edition

RAISING BIG SMILING TENNIS KIDS

Whether you are a tennis playing parent or a parent curious about tennis, this book will empower you to raise kids who swing the tennis racket with as much aplomb as their happy smiles.

The best age to get your kid started in tennis. How to motivate kids to go back, practice after practice. When to focus exclusively on tennis. Save on lessons, find scholarships and sponsors. How to pursue a career in professional tennis. Gain insight into tennis organizations and agents. Have fun along the way at the best tennis camps and resort

TENNIS BEYOND BIG SHOTS

Win BIG with Small Changes! A book for every tennis enthusiast. Tennis Beyond Big Shots presents a bold back-to-the-future approach.

A new game that moves away from power and big shots yet is more lethal to opponents than any booming serve.

Forgotten shots that will raise your game. Why good thinking tops great strokes? Secrets of the new "power game" to win, play and enjoy more

ISBN 1932421041
First Edition

ISBN 1932421149
First Edition

GOLF GUIDE FOR PARENTS AND PLAYERS

Jack Nicklaus acclaimed guide unveils the secrets of success for junior and college golf, the professional tour and beyond.

Golf pros Jacqui and Johnny, offer exclusive guidance and new ideas on: How to motivate kids to go back, practice after practice. When to focus exclusively on golf. Save on lessons, find scholarships and sponsors. How to pursue college golf and a career in professional golf. Gain insight into golf organizations and agents. Have fun along the way at the best golf camps and resorts.

RAISING BIG SMILING SQUASH KIDS

Stanford University recently added Squash to its athletics, joining Yale and Cornell. Forbes magazine rates Squash as the number one sport for fitness. With courts and college programs springing up across the country.

Richard Millman, world-class coach and Georgetta Morque, a prolific sportswriter, offer a complete roadmap for parents, professionals and kids. The best age to get started in squash; how to motivate kids; the road to top colleges; and attractive career options. Plus: cultivating friendships, character building and achieving a lifetime of fitness.

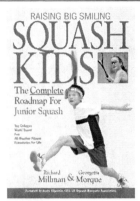

ISBN 1932421432
2006 First Edition

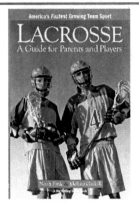

ISBN 1932421076
2006 First Edition

LACROSSE: A GUIDE FOR PARENTS AND PLAYERS

Lacrosse is America's fastest growing team sport. Action-packed and fun, lacrosse is a game anyone can play — the big and small, boys and girls. Lacrosse offers a positive outlet, a place to fit in at school, motivation to excel, and opportunities for team travel.

Whether your kid is 8 or 18, experienced or just starting, this book is the complete guide to all that lacrosse has to offer. Empower yourself with practical answers and unique ideas, whether you are new to lacrosse or once were a player. Make lacrosse an exhilarating part of your family life.

AVAILABLE WORLDWIDE

INTRODUCING
Racket Bracket®
The Fastest Way to Improve Your Game!

The Racket Bracket is a revolutionary tennis training aid engineered to allow just the right amount of wrist flexibility to execute a perfect swing. It is an incredible coaching and learning aid for volleys, slices, and groundstrokes. The Racket Bracket is endorsed by Ellis Ferreira, winner of two Grand Slam titles.

MANSION
SELECT

QuickStart Tennis Systems, Innovative Tennis Training Aids Plus!
Quality Tennis Gear, Apparel, Videos, Books, Gifts & More
Carefully Selected For Tennis Pros, Moms, Dads, Kids, & Players
Visit Today!

MansionSelect.com
Ph: 512.366.9012 ✦ Fax: 512.366.9012
Institutional Orders Fax: 512.366.9012

Printed in the United States
103420LV00006B/1-42/P